Re-Reading the Old Testament Prophets

Biblical Hermeneutics Rediscovered

The Series as the name suggests will focus on Biblical Hermeneutics, i.e., literary works concerned with methods of interpreting the Old and New Testaments of Bible via different stream of topics like Literature & Poetry, Indigenous Philosophizing, Ethical response towards Ecology, Health & Healing, Science & Technology, Feminist Theology, Sociological approach towards Human Rights, Law & Politics, Arts, History of Ideas, Ancient Civilizations, Cultural Contiguity, Religious Cosmologies & Mysticism, Appraisal of various Theologians, World Peace & Harmony, Global Capitalism, Network Marketing, Cybertheology, Population & Demographics, Epigraphic Studies, Contextualized Education, and many others. We welcome a Mss. on any topic/s mentioned, whether they are original works, scholarly monographs, collections of conference papers, revised dissertations, or translations of historical documents. Through the Series we, the Publishers, are striving to put forward published works that may help Institutions, Academic Bodies, Researchers, Scholars and the World at large in furthering their respective knowledge and understanding on the concerned subject. We welcome your comments on our efforts and further suggestions on how we can enshrine new ray of analysing & explaining the written Texts through our upcoming books.

Biblical Hermeneutics Rediscovered - 20

Re-Reading the Old Testament Prophets

The Spirit of God in the Exilic Seers

B. Lalnunzira

CWI

Christian World Imprints

First Published in 2019 by

Christian World Imprints
Christian Publishing & Books from India
H-12 Bali Nagar, **New Delhi-110015**
info@christianworldimprints.com
www.ChristianWorldImprints.com
Phone: +91 11 25465925

ISBN: 978-93-5148-354-0 (HB)
ISBN: 978-93-5148-355-7 (PB)

Printed in India.

Contents

The book in its original form is the thesis submitted to the Senate of Serampore College towards Master of Theology (MTh) degree and published it with permission from the Senate. The author is responsible for the contents, ideas and opinions expressed in the book. The title of the book is reframed to the present form for the purpose of publication.

Preface

This book is a study of the understanding of the Spirit of God in the writings of the Exilic Prophets. It seeks to explore how exilic prophets such as Ezekiel, Deutero-Isaiah, and Jeremiah construe the meaning, significance, and operation of the Spirit of God in the context of the Babylonian Exile of the sixth century BCE. As a backdrop, the book discusses how other books of the Old Testament portray the Spirit of God in different situations. The book brings out interpretation of the spirit (*ruah*) of God in different contexts and how the exilic prophets domesticate the role and function of the Spirit of God in a particular time and space, which is the Babylonian imperial domination. Hence, it is a rereading of the Old Testament Prophets in general and the Exilic Seers in particular. The book shows that the understanding of the Spirit of God developed over a period of time in the Old Testament period. It is evident that the Spirit of God operated contextually as portrayed by biblical authors, including the Exilic Prophets. The book intimates interpreters a possibility to bring out contextual pneumatology.

I thank Mr. Sudhanshu Kanda and the team of Christian World Imprints (CWI) for their efforts in publishing this book. I hope and pray that this humble work will contribute to understand how Biblical texts have meaning and significance in specific contexts.

List of Abbreviations

ABD	-	Anchor Bible Dictionary
ANET	-	Ancient Near Eastern Texts Relating to the Old Testament
BCE	-	Before Common Era
BHS	-	Biblia Hebraica Stuttgartensia
CBQ	-	Catholic Bible Quarterly
Cf.	-	Compare with
Chaps	-	Chapters
HALOT	-	Hebrew and Aramaic Lexicon of the Old Testament
ICC	-	International Critical Commentary
ISBE	-	International Standard Bible Encyclopaedia
JBL	-	Journal of Biblical Literature
JSOT	-	Journal for the Study of the Old Testament
KJV	-	King James Version
LXX	-	Septuagint
MT	-	Masoretic Text
NAC	-	New American Commentary
NCB	-	New Century Bible

NEB	-	New English Bible
NICOT	-	New International Commentary of the Old Testament
NIDOTTE	-	New International Dictionary of Old Testament Theology and Exegesis
NIV	-	New International Version
NJB	-	New Jerusalem Bible
NRSV	-	New Revised Standard Version
p, pp	-	page, pages
RSV	-	Revised Standard Version
TDNT	-	Theological Dictionary of the New Testament
TDOT	-	Theological Dictionary of the Old Testament
TLOT	-	Theological Lexicon of the Old Testament
v, vv	-	verse, verses
WBC	-	Word Biblical Commentary
ZAW	-	Zeitschrift Fier Die Alttestamentliche Wissenschft

Introduction

1. The Research Question

The Old Testament contains a number of references to the "Spirit of God" in different forms. A cursory survey of the Old Testament shows that the understanding of the Spirit of God seems to be divergent in different books of the Old Testament. The most popular term used to refer spirit in the Old Testament is *ruah*. The term is used most frequently to mean 'power or spirit.' However, it has variety of meaning such as "wind," "breathe," "life" etc. Even when applied to God, it seems to signify various connotations.

Interestingly, prophetic literature of the exilic period represents quite a number of statements about the Spirit of God.[1] Traces of peculiar usage of the Spirit of God may be noticed in this prophetic literature as we compare with other Old Testament books. While the Spirit of God is no more associated with the succeeding kings after David, the exilic prophets associated the Spirit of God with kingship (Isa. 42:1ff.). While pre-exilic reforming prophets normally

[1] To ascertain the number of exilic prophets is difficult with precision. However, Jeremiah, Ezekiel, and Deutero-Isaiah are generally known as exilic prophets. See Ralph W. Klein, *Israel in Exile* (Philadelphia: Fortress Press, 1979), 152. Also, see Walter Brueggemann, *Hopeful Imagination: Prophetic Voice in Exile* (Philadelphia: Fortress Press, 1986), 1.

never speak of the possession of the *spirit* in order to justify or authenticate their vision,[2] the Spirit of God is portrayed as an inspiring force in the exilic prophets (Ezek. 11:4-6; Isa. 48:16). A distinctive understanding of the Spirit of God seems to be appeared in the prophetic literature as the term spirit seems to connote a person (Isa. 48:16). New concepts seem to have been developed in this time as the Spirit of God appears to be a permanent gift (Ezek. 36:27), having universal significance (Isa. 44:1-5); and it seems to be associated with eschatological element as it will be poured upon the house/seed of Israel (Isa.43: 3; Ezek.39: 29). A new role is seemingly given to the Spirit of God, as endowment of the spirit signifies giving new life and restoration (Ezek. 37: 14). The significance of the Spirit of God in the exilic prophet is well attested as even some scholars find continuity of the exilic (and post-exilic) prophetic understanding of the Spirit of God in the New Testament.[3]

The above particular features demand serious inquiries into the following questions: What is the Spirit of God in the Old Testament, and what is it's meaning in the exilic prophets? Is the Spirit of God a mere breathe of God or God's powerful agent that manifested as wind? Is it a person or dynamic power of God? Why is it so significant in the writings of the exilic prophets? Why do the exilic prophets associate the Spirit of God with certain elements that are absent in the pre-exilic period? Do the exilic prophets develop the understanding of the Spirit of God as a response to the exilic experience? Will the political, socio-economic and religious contexts of the exile give new meaning and significance to the Spirit of God? Could there be a specific theological motivation behind the meaning and significance of the Spirit of God in the exilic prophetic literature? Therefore, the purpose in this study is to investigate the meaning and significance of the Spirit of God in the writings of the exilic prophets.

---

[2] Edmond Jacob, *Theology of the Old Testament*, translated by Arthur. W. Heathcote and Philip J. Allcock. (London: Hodder & Stoughton 1958), 125.

[3] See Rainer Albertz and Claus Westermann, "רוח," *TLOT* Vol-3, edited by Ernst Jenni & Claus Westermann, translated by Mark E. Biddle. (Massachusetts: Hendrickson Publishers, 1977), 1220.

2. Survey of Previous Research

A review of the previous research on the subject reveals that most of the studies done by scholars are general survey on the understanding of the Spirit of God and so far no specific study was done on the meaning and significance of the Spirit of God in the writings of the exilic prophets. However, there are some works generally related to the study in various forms. Walter Eichrodt in his Theology of the Old Testament Vol. II surveys the meaning and function of the Spirit (*spirit*) of God under the title "The Cosmic Power of God" in which four main features of the meaning and functions of the Spirit of God are narrated.[4] William Dyrness in Themes in Old Testament Theology traces the theological development of the Spirit of God. However, a detailed study on the exilic prophets is not done.[5] Important works on the subject are also seen in An Outlines of Old Testament Theology by Th. C. Vriezen;[6] The Distinctive Ideas of the Old Testament by Norman H. Snaith.[7] A study on the term "*Spirit*" and "the Spirit of God" are seen in Lexicons and Dictionaries.[8] The role of the Spirit of God in exilic period is dealt with by Richard J. Sklba in his article entitled "Until the Spirit from on High is Poured Out on Us (Isa. 32:15): Reflections of the Role of the Spirit in the

---

[4] See Walther Eichrodt, *Theology of the Old Testament,* Vol. II (London: SCM Press Ltd., 1967), 46-68.

[5] William Dyrness, *Themes in Old Testament Theology* (Downers Grove, Illinois: InterVarsity Press, 1979), 201-209.

[6] Th. C. Vriezen, *An Outline of Old Testament Theology* (Oxford: Basil Blackwell, 1970), 211-216.

[7] Norman H. Snaith, *The Distinctive Ideas of the Old Testament.* (London: The Epworth Press, 1953), 143-158.

[8] For example Rainer Albertz and Claus Westermann, "רוח," *TLOT* Vol-3 edited by Ernst Jenni & Claus Westermann, translated by Mark E. Biddle. (Massachusetts: Hendrickson Publishers, 1977), 1202-1220. Baumgartel, "Spirit in the Old Testament" *TDNT* Vol. 6, edited by Gerhard Friederich, translated by Geoffrey E. Bromiley (Grand Rapids, Michigan: Eerdmans, 1968), 359-368. M.V. Vanpelt, W.C. Kaiser Jr. and D.I. Block, "רוח" *NIDOTTE* Vol-3, edited by William A. van Gemeren et. al., (UK: Paternoster Press, 1996), 1073-1078.

Exile."[9] This article surveys the development of the concept in the time of the exilic and postexilic age, as reflected from the perspectives of royal theologies, prophetic theologies, and rural theologies. According to Sklba, the functions of the Spirit during the exilic period were determined by variety of thoughts derived from various sources. However, a special treatment on the prophets is lacking. M. R. Westhall who works on "The Scope of the Spirit of God in the Old Testament" suggests a debatable conclusion that the Spirit of God in the Old Testament is predominantly the transcendent power of God at work upon selected individuals and not necessarily a moral power.[10]

The above studies on the Spirit of God are mainly general surveys, and so far a particular treatment on the prophetic literature of the exilic age in relation to the meaning and significance of the Spirit of God is not done in any form. Moreover, an investigation on the socio-political and religious context of the exile, which may possibly be the factor behind the understanding of the Spirit of God, had not been taken up seriously. Thus, this study would be one of the initial attempts to specifically investigate the meaning and significance of the Spirit of God in the writings of the exilic prophets.

3. Scope

Since the study is an investigation of the meaning and significance of the Spirit of God in the writings of the exilic prophets, the main concern is an exegetical study of relevant passages of the exilic prophets. Only passages relevant to our theme are chosen for exegetical analysis. Since the study deals with the phrase "the Spirit of God," a philological study of the term *ruah* and its cognate terms. Also a brief sketch on the distinction between Spirit of Yahweh and Spirit Elohim will be taken care. A brief survey of the usage of *spirit* and the Spirit of God will be taken up as one of the preliminary concerns. Since the study is concentrated on the writings of the

[9] Richard J. Sklba, "Until the Spirit from on high is pour out on us (Isa. 32:15): Reflections of the Role of the Spirit in the Exile" *The Catholic Bible Quarterly* 46/1 (January, 1984): 1-17.

[10] M. R. Westall, "The Scope of the term Spirit of God in the Old Testament" *Indian Journal of Theology* 26/1 (January, 1977): 29-43.

exilic prophets, an investigation of the *sitz-im-leben* of the exilic community and prophetic response of the situations is also taken up in the study. Passages for exegesis are limited to nine passages, five from Ezekiel, three from Deutero-Isaiah, and one from the book of Jeremiah, to represent the writings of exilic prophets.

4. Method

The method applied in the study is mainly exegetical. In the research, relevant passages are dealt with by making use of various critical tools. Basically, the form-critical, tradition-historical method and textual analysis is applied in the appropriate context. Since the understanding of the Spirit of God was originated and developed by the Israelite community and transmitted to later generations of the community through a long process, and since the prophets to a certain extent bear witness to this process of transmission, the form critical analysis is given priority as the exegetical tool.[11] In order to help the exegesis, a philological study and general survey of the Old Testament understanding of the "Spirit of God" are taken up. Also a study of the political, socio-economic and religious contexts of the exilic prophets and prophetic response to the situations is taken up as a background study.

5. Structure

The study begins with an introduction, which provides the problem to be investigated, a review of previous research, scope and method of the research, structure and format of the thesis. The first chapter deals with the Spirit of God in the Old Testament, in which a philological study of the term, the usage of *spirit* and the Spirit of God, and a brief survey of the development of the understanding of the Spirit of God in the Old Testament are dealt with. The second chapter concentrates on an investigation on the political, socio-economic

---

[11] According to Gene M. Tucker, there are four basic steps of Form critical method of exegesis such as: (1) Analysis of the structure, (2) description of the genre, (3) definition of the setting or settings, and (4) statement of indication, purpose or function of the text. See *Form Criticism of the Old Testament* (Philadelphia: Fortress Press, 1971), 11.

and religious contexts of the exilic age and prophetic response to the then situations.

Chapter three, four, and five are exegetical studies of relevant passages found in the book of Ezekiel, Deutero-Isaiah, and Jeremiah. Since Ezekiel contains more passages relating to the Spirit of God, it is firstly dealt with in the exegesis as found in chapter three. This is followed by Deutero-Isaiah in the fourth chapter. Chapter five deals with Jeremiah's distinctive use of the spirit in relation to God and an implicit use of the Spirit of God in the book. However, a parallel reference of the passage to the Spirit of God is also looked upon. The final concluding remarks provide a summary from all the previous chapters. It also summarizes the findings of the research. Attempt is also made to see how far the study is relevant for formulation of contextual pneumatology.

6. Format of the Investigation

The format of the investigation runs as follows: After background studies in chapter one and two, exegetical study follows. A brief introduction is made in each of the chapter, which deals with authorship, composition and specific notes on particular prophets. The exegetical study proceeds as follows: After translation of the selected texts, a text critical notes follows. This is followed by a form critical analysis. Here, the plausible reason for isolating a given text based on its structure and genre is examined. Questions of the setting including authorship is dealt with which is followed by comments in relation to the meaning and significance of the Spirit of God. Each chapter is concluded with a brief summary. The last part of the study synthesizes the studies by proposing how the study could be implied for formulation of contextual pneumatology.

Chapter 1

The Spirit of God in the Old Testament

1.1. Introduction

The Old Testament contains a number of references to the "Spirit (רוח)[12] of God" either in the form of Spirit of Yahweh or Spirit of Elohim or the Spirit or represented with suffixes and adjectives. Traces of different meanings and significance are to be noted in the use of the term Spirit of God in different books of the Old Testament. The Hebrew root for spirit is *ruah*. It has many secular meanings such as wind, breath, passion, thought, and the self.[13] In the Old Testament, spirit is primarily the prerogative of God. When the term is used in connection with God, the dynamic power and life giving force is primarily mentioned. Having diverse meaning and significations, proper treatment of the meaning of spirit in general and the Spirit of God in particular demands serious inquiry. This chapter therefore, deals with an etymological study of the term *ruah*,

---

[12] The Hebrew "רוח" is represented in its transliteration as *ruah* in this book.

[13] Th. C. Vriezen, *An Outline of Old Testament Theology* (Oxford: Basil Blackwell, 1970), 212.

its cognate terms and various usages of *ruah* and the *ruah* (spirit) of God. A survey of the conceptual development of the Spirit of God in the Old Testament is also dealt with in this discussion.

1.2. Etymological Study

The Hebrew word *ruah* (רוח), which is most frequently translated as "spirit," is a relative term which could have diverse meaning. It occurs 378 times in the Old Testament and 11 times in the Aramaic.[14] Kohler and Baumgartner find 387 occurrences in the Old Testament.[15] The etymological meaning of the term may come from Semitic root *rh,* which signifies "to breathe" or "to blow."[16] The Aramaic *rwh* means "wind/spirit;" the Akkadian *rih* means, "wind" and, *saru* means, "wind or breath."[17] In Arabic, *raha* means "to blow," *rih-* means "wind," and *ruh* means "spirit."[18] Kindred word in Hebrew רֵיחַ means "scent," or odour; which comes from the verb רִיחַ (only in hiphil) "to smell," "to perceive."[19] The verb רָוַח (Qal) means "to be wide" or "to be spacious;" and רֶוַח (ptc.) means space or interval.[20] Perhaps the kindred words in Hebrew are associated with the root *rh* to connote smelling as breath or be spacious as wind operates.

[14] Rainer Albertz and Claus Westermann, "רוח," *TLOT* Vol-3, edited by Ernst Jenni & Claus Westermann, translated by Mark E. Biddle (Massachusetts: Hendrickson Publishers, 1977), 1207. (Hereafter "רוח," *TLOT*).

[15] The term is not found in Leviticus, Obadiah, Nahum, Ruth, Esther and Song of Songs. See Ludwig Kohler and Walter Baumgartner, "רוח" *Hebrew and Aramaic Lexicon of the Old Testament* Vol.2., translated and edited by M.E.J. Richardson (Leiden: Brill, 2000), 1197. (Hereafter Kohler and Baumgartner, "רוח," *HALOT*).

[16] R. Birch Hoyle, "Spirit (Holy Spirit), Spirit of God" *Encyclopedia of Religion and Ethics* Vol. XI, edited by James Hastings et. al., (1920): 784-785.

[17] Albertz and Claus Westermann, "רוח," *TLOT* Vol-3, 1203.

[18] Fredrich Baumgartel, "רוח," in the OT," *TDNT* Vol. 6, edited by Gerhard Friedrich, translated and edited in English by G.W. Bromiley (Grand Rapids, Michigan: Eerdmans, 1968), 360. (Hereafter Baumgartel, "Spirit in the Old Testament" *TDNT*).

[19] Francis Brown, S.R. Driver & Charles A Briggs, *A Hebrew and English Lexicon of the Old Testament* (Oxford: Clarendon Press, 1968), 924. (Hereafter Brown Driver Briggs, *Lexicon*).

[20] Brown Driver Briggs, *Lexicon*, 926.

Thus, the primary meaning of *ruah* (noun feminine) appears to be air in motion as wind or breath. The general idea of its meaning is power in manifestation, or energy."[21] It is the power of movement and activity, the power of life and vitality.[22] Albertz and Westermann, however, say that the term is not understood as an essence; but rather it is the power encountered in the breath and in the wind; whose whence and whither remains mysterious.[23] Therefore, on account of the wide range of its meaning, the acceptable definition of spirit is extremely difficult.

Kamlah observes that *ruah* is both the extraordinary movement of something that is tangible and the effects of such movement."[24] It is likely that from a literal meaning of *ruah* as wind or breath, a highly developed religious idea of spirit emerged.[25] The literal meaning of *ruah* as air in motion or breath becomes a significant term for "spirit" as power in motion of life-giving force. Thus, the etymological meaning of the term *ruah* as wind or breath has also become a religious term for spirit in the Old Testament.

The Greek equivalent for *ruah*, found in the Septuagint is *pneuma* F. Arndt and F. Wilbur Gingrich define *pneuma* as: (1) wind – blowing and breathing; (2) breath of life (3) spirit as a part of human personality; (4) spirit – as an independent being; (5) the Spirit of God (as distinct from others); (6) the Divine spirit

---

[21] According to A.R. Johnson etymologically, in all the eastern branch of the Semitic languages, the term spirit refers to an initial awareness of air in motion, particularly wind. See *Vitality of the Individual in the Thought of Ancient Israel* (Cardiff: University of Wales Press, 1964), 23.

[22] See more detailed study of the etymological meaning in J.R. John Samuel Raj, "Spirit and Kingship in the Old Testament" Unpublished BD Thesis (Bangalore: UTC, 1983), 5.

[23] Albertz. & Westermann, "רוח" *TLOT*, 1203.

[24] Cited in M.V. Vanpelt, W.C. Kaiser Jr. and D.I. Block, "רוח" *NIDOTTE* Vol-3, edited by William A. van Gemeren et.al (UK: Paternoster Press, 1996), 1073. (Hereafter "רוח" *NIDOTTE*).

[25] Wonsuk Ma, "The Spirit (Spirit of God) in Isaiah 1-39," *Asian Journal of Theology* 3/2 (October, 1989): 583.

which indwells in humans; (7); a spirit against Spirit of God; (8) independent personality.[26]

1.3. Cognate Terms

In the Old Testament we encounter certain terms which are more or less related to the term רוח (spirit). Sometimes, they are used synonymously or sometimes in parallel to the term רוח. Important to be noted among which are: נשמה (*N^e^shama*), and נפש (*Nephesh*).

1.3.1 נשמה (*N^e^shmah*)

A feminine form of the root נשם literally means, "to pant" "to breath" or "to blow."[27] The term is found 24 times in its noun form and once in its verbal form in the Old Testament.[28] The use of the term is also attested beyond biblical Hebrew. The basic meaning of the term is "breath," "wind," also "breath of life" or "living creature." The meaning and its usage in the Old Testament may be broadly defined as follows:[29] (1) Breath in general (Isa. 2:22), (2) breath of human that gives life to the body (Gen. 3:27), (3) life in general (I Kings 17:17), (4) living creatures (Deut. 20:8), God's *n^e^shama* is depicted as a life-giving breath or the vital force that God gives (Job 27:3). Looking from the usages mentioned above, the most common connotation of *n^e^shama* may be breath in humans as well as creative breath of God.[30]

One significant usage of *n^e^shama* is its use in relation to spirit (*ruah).* Spirit appears as its parallel in certain passages (cf. Eccl.

[26] F. Arndt and F. Wilbur Gingrich, *A Greek English Lexicon of the New Testament and Other Early Christian Literature* (Chicago: The University of Chicago Press, 1979), 674-678.

[27] Brown Briggs and Driver, *Lexicon*, 675.

[28] It is distributed in the Old Testament (Hebrew) as: Pentateuch-3, Deuteronomic History-6, Prophets (Isaiah)- 4 and Wisdom Literature-11 times. It occurs once each in Aramaic (Dan. 5:23 and Sirach 1:13). See Lamberty-Zielinski, "נשמה" *TDOT* Vol. X, edited by G. Johannes Botterweck, Heinz-Josef Fabry, translated by Douglas W. Stott (Grand Rapids, Michigan: Eerdmans, 1998), 66.

[29] For detailed study see Koehler and Baumgartner, *HALOT*, 730, also Baumgartel, "רוח" in the OT," *TDNT,* 364.

[30] Cf. D.C. Fredericks, "נְשָׁמָה," *NIDOTTE* Vol. 3, 190.

12:7) or used synonymous with each other (Gen. 7:22; II Sam. 22:16). However, A.R. Johnson argues that the use does not seem to have common before the exile and that the great prophets of exile employed the two terms synonymously.[31] The relationship between the two terms is defined that the spirit is found in all creatures and the sign of the spirit in creatures is *n^e^shama* (breath). The Old Testament portrays that if the spirit is in a being, there is *n^e^shama* in it, and hence it has life and soul. Therefore, *n^e^shama* is a breath of life, the effect of spirit given to human by God, to make him/her alive.

1.3.2. נפש (*Nephesh*)

The Hebrew root נפש has counterparts in all Semitic languages and the various meanings that Hebrew נֶפֶשׁ exhibits also occur for the most part in related languages.[32] The term occurs 757 times in the Hebrew Old Testament (501 in singular and 51 in plural form).[33] Basically the word refers to a particular part of the body that is the neck, throat/gullet, as the organ through which one breathes.[34] Others see "the act of breathing" as the primary detonation of the term.[35] One could have assumed that *nephes* primarily stands at the same time for the organ through which one breathes, and for the

---

[31] A.R. Johnson, *Vitality of the Individual*, 27ff.

[32] Examples are Akkadian "*napistu*" which means throat/life, Amorites "*napsh*"- breath/life, Ugarit "*nps*"- throat/appetite, soul, living being, etc. See Claus Westermann, "נֶפֶשׁ" *TLOT* Vol. 2, 743.

[33] Seebas, " נֶפֶשׁ," *TDOT* Vol. IX, 502.

[34] Walter Eichrodt, *Theology of the Old Testament* Vol. II, translated by J.A. Backer (London: SCM Press Ltd, 1967), 134.

[35] Vriezen, J.H. Becker, D. Lys, and J.H. Scheepers advocate this thesis. See Th. C. Vriezen, *An Outline of Old Testament Theology*, 407. See also detailed study on the meaning and usage of *nephes* in the Old Testament in Nitoy K. Achumi, "The Meaning and the Use of *Nephes* in the Old Testament and Its Translation into the Sema Naga Bible" (Unpublished M. Th. Thesis. Bangalore: UTC, 1975).

act of breathing.[36] נֶפֶשׁ of God is rarely used in the Old Testament.[37] The use of in the Old Testament may be described as follows: (1) the organ of eating and breathing (Isa. 5:14), (2) a vital force which is in animate forms of life, and (3) soul or vital self, a relationship with oneself (Deut. 4:29).

The relationship of *nephes* to the concept of spirit may be defined that *nephes* is understood as the life that is in human, and spirit as the life force working in all creatures that have a body. Therefore, they are not separate elemental components of humans, but are manifestations of vitality.[38] However, distinction could be made that *nephes* is the individual life in association with a body, and spirit is supra-individual in character, the life force present everywhere and existing independently over against the single individual.[39] A distinction could be made that *nephes* is a life in an individual that comes to an end with the death of the individual. On the other hand, spirit is universal, and independent of the death of the creature.

1.4. Different Usages of *Ruah*

As pointed out in the above, the most popular term for spirit- *ruah* has several meanings. Being distributed widely in different books of the Bible including in the Law (*Torah*), Prophets (*Nebiim*) and the Writings (*Ketubim*), the term could have signified divine quality, natural force and the life-force in human being, etc. Now we will look upon different usages of *ruah* in the Old Testament.

---

[36] This is one of the characters of Hebrew synthetic thinking according to which a part of the body and its functions are one. See H.W. Robinson, "Hebrew Psychology" in *The People and the Book*, edited by A.S. Peake (Oxford: Clarendon Press, nd.), 18.

[37] A small group of passages portray God's aversion to his people with such intensity and passion that God's *nephesh* is the subject of the act (Jer. 5:9, 29; 6:8; 9:8; 14:19 cf. Lev. 26:11,30; Isa. 1:14; Ezek. 28:18; Zech. 11:8). This group of texts describe God's passionate aversion to his people in prophetic language (all except Lev. 26) with *nephesh* as the subject, This description indicates that *nephesh* is not something that pertains to people (or God) or is in people, but the intensity of a behaviour or feeling is the indication. See Westermann, "נפשׁ," *TLOT*, 757.

[38] Pezhumkattil, "Anthropological Concept of the Old Testament," *Bible Bhashyam* XVIII/1 (March, 1992): 8.

[39] Eichrodt, *Theology of the Old Testament* II, 136.

1.4.1. *Ruah* as Wind

According to Wolf, *ruah* is to a large extent the term for a natural power, or the wind. This meaning is applied in no less than 113 out of 389 (387+11) instances.[40] Albertz and Westermann explain that the Old Testament observes the wind (*ruah*) in its real physical manifestations. On the other hand, it relates it, to a greater or lesser degree, to Yahweh.[41] *Ruah* as an independent physical manifestation is at the same time the powerful agent of God Normally, it denotes movement of air, mostly destructive, strong and violent (Ex. 10:13; Num. 11:31; Ps.1: 4). In a derived sense, *ruah* is also used of as the four compass points, which is implied in "to every wind" (Ezek. 5:10-12), "the four winds" (Jer 49:36). For the author of Ecclesiastes the pursuit of fleeting pleasures is vanity, a "chasing after the *ruah* (wind)"[42] *Ruah* as wind, a physical reality is always closely associated with God. It is one of his best servants (Ps. 104:4); it dried up the sea and gave Israelites passage (Ex. 14:21; Gen 8:1). It comes from Yahweh's agency or breaks forth from him (Jer. 4:12; Num 11:31). God's activity and the wind's action occasionally appear together almost self-evidently (Ex. 21:25; Ezek. 13:11, 13). Thus, *ruah* signifies the movement of air as controlled by God.

1.4.2. *Ruah* as Breath

The second basic meaning of *ruah* is "breath" not as a constant phenomenon but as a force expressed in respiration. It does not indicate "normal breathing" a component of human life (*n^e^shama*), but the particular process of breathing that expresses the human being's vitality.[43] Edmond Jacob indicates that *ruah* denotes the

---

[40] Hans Walter Wolf, *Anthropology of the Old Testament* (Philadelphia: Fortress Press, 1974), 32. The Number of the term signifying wind could not be ascertained because it is not certain what the term *ruah* refers to in certain passages. For example Gen. 1:2 could be interpreted either as wind or spirit. See discussion in this problem in M. R. Westall "The Scope of the Term 'Spirit of God' in the Old Testament" *Indian Journal of Theology* 26/1 (January, 1977): 31-32.

[41] Albertz and Westermann, "רוח," *TLOT*, 1205.

[42] Cf. Eccl. 1:6, 14, 17; 2:11, 17, 26; 4:4, 6, 16; 6:9.

[43] Albertz and Westermann, "רוח," *TLOT*, 1207.

breath of life which is in effect the breath of God.[44] This idea of breath of life as an effect of the breath of God is common in ANE religions.[45] It stands for the hard, strong and violent breathing, as against *n^eshama*, an ordinary breathing.[46] The distinctive use of *ruah* as breath could be observed in different passages. There is no spirit in the idols of wood or stone (Hab. 2:19; Jer. 10:14); that is to say, they have no breath and therefore no vital power. When spirit departs he/she (human) returns to earth (Ps. 146:4). Numerous texts in the Old Testament affirm that the breath of God is life giving.[47] The Old Testament attests that the spirit (breath) on the whole always remains the property of God, which is free at any instant to take it back to him/herself.[48] Thus, *ruah* is known as breath of life; a principle of life in all creatures. The breath (*ruah*) of God enters into a creature through the direct action of God and this is known as the Spirit of God in that man (sic).[49] Therefore, one can conclude that *ruah* is used to refer to the breath of life in human being, which is in the effect and control of God.

1.4.3. *Ruah* as Feeling

Ruah is also interpreted as feeling in some instances denoting a person's or group's disposition, attitude, mood or inclination. Snaith takes the usage of *ruah* in the realm of psychology to denote the dominant impulse or disposition of an individual.[50] These are

---

[44] Edmond Jacob, *Theology of the Old Testament*, translated by Arthur. W. Heathcote and Philip J. Allcock (London: Hodder & Stoughton 1958), 122.

[45] The idea is common among the Egyptians, Babylonians, Assyrians, Phoenicians, Canaanites and Hebrews. See Edmond Jacob, *Theology of the Old Testament*, 122; also Eichrodt, *Theology of the Old Testament* II, 47.

[46] The term though distinct from *neshama* is used ten times in connection with it and it and can be used to refer to the life-sustaining function. See Snaith, *The Distinctive Ideas of the Old Testament*, (London: Epworth Press, 1962), 144.

[47] Cf. Gen. 6:17; 7:15; Num. 16:22; Judg. 15:19; Ps. 104:29; Eccl. 3:1; 9:21; 12:7; Isa. 37:6, 8; Zech 21:1.

[48] See Edmond Jacob, *Theology of the Old Testament,* 122.

[49] See discussion in Pezhumkattil, *Anthropological Concept of the Old Testament*, 10.

[50] Snaith, *Distinctive Ideas of the Old Testament*, 146.

typically constructed by appropriate adjectives such as a bitter *ruah* (Gen. 26:35), anger (Ezek. 3:14), a short *ruah* (Exod. 6:9), a trustworthy spirit (Prov. 11:13), etc. In this regard Wolf defines *ruah* as organ of knowledge, understanding and judgment seen together with the movement of feelings.[51] Thus, *ruah* can be described as the entire range of human frames of mind, from the strongest emotions to the failure of all vitality.

1.4.4. *Ruah* as Will

Ruah as will has led us beyond the sense of spirit as an attitude of mind, in which it is largely related in meaning to *nephes*. It points to a focal point of a whole range of psychical activity, the seat of cognition and volition, those activities involved in thinking, aptitude and decision-making.[52] The usage of *ruah* in this case has frequent contact with that of *leb* (heart),[53] which designates originally an organ (heart) but can be expanded to a focal point of a whole range of psychical activity.[54] Thus will and heart stands for seat of understanding which stands for that of an individual, which dominates him/her so as to ensure particular type of action. It designates reason (Job 32:8), extraordinary cleverness (Dan. 6:4), artistic sense (Ex. 28:3), fullness of thoughts (Job 32:15), and planning (I Chro. 28:12). *Ruah* as will is frequently described to be endowed by the Spirit of God (I Sam 16:14ff; 18:10; 19:9). Thus, Ezekiel predicts that Yahweh will give his people a "new heart" and a "new spirit " (spirit/will) that they may obey his law (Ezek. 36:26).

---

[51] Wolf, *Anthropology of the Old Testament*, 36.

[52] See detailed discussion in Albertz and Westermann, "רוח," *TLOT*, 1210, A clear example of this usage is seen in Ezra 1:5 which speaks of: "whose *ruah* God had stirred to go up to rebuild the house of Yahweh in Jerusalem." Here it is the will that *ruah* stands for. Wolf, *Anthropology of the Old Testament*, 38.

[53] It is acknowledged that in 21 instances *ruah* and *leb* occur together as synonymous of one another. See M.V. Vanpelt, W.C. Kaiser Jr. and D.I. Block in "ruah," *NIDOTTE*, 1075.

[54] A. R. Johnson, *Vitality of the Individual*, 76.

1.4.5. *Ruah* as Spirit: Life-giving Force

As we have discussed, *ruah* is the life-giving force, a controlling element in human being. It is therefore, a determining force in human being. In this case *ruah* may be called as spirit in/of human being. It is also to be noted that this controlling spirit is other than the person him/herself, as if a controlling and dominating power from outside. In this case *ruah* may be termed as the Spirit of God. Thus, the spirit of human and Spirit of God are interrelated; and it is extremely difficult to determine whether in certain passages in the book of the Old Testament (and the New Testament) the reference is to the Spirit of God or the spirit of human.[55] *Spirit* becomes the sign and principle of vitality itself; it is the unseen spiritual element in human being, which is called spirit in human.[56] The Bible talks of the spirit of Moses (Dt. 34:9), the spirit of Elijah (II Kings 2:9), etc. The Bible makes it clear that human being is a flesh, made from the dust of the earth, animated by *ruah* (spirit) so that he is a *nephes* (living being). Snaith argues that the use of *ruah* to indicate the Spirit of God is markedly distinct neither terminologically nor materially from the profane usage.[57] The vital power (spirit) that comes from God is at the same time the breath and vital power (spirit) by which all creatures live. A.B. Davidson defines the Spirit of God as:

> The spirit in/of God *ab intra* is God active, showing life and power, of the kinds similar to those exhibited by the spirit of man (sic) in man (sic); that the Spirit of God *ab extra* is God in efficient operation, whether in the cosmos or as giving life, reinforcing life, exerting efficiency in any sphere, according to the nature of the sphere, whether physical, intellectual or spiritual; and that the tendency towards limiting the Spirit of God to the ethical and spiritual spheres is due to those sides of His being.[58]

---

[55] G.W.H. Lampe, *God as Spirit* (Oxford: Clarendon Press, 1977), 45.

[56] A.B. Davidson, *The Theology of the Old Testament* (Edinburgh: T&T Clark, 1907), 195.

[57] Snaith finds some 25 cases where *ruah* is used in equivalent with *nephes*. See *Distinctive Ideas of the Old Testament*, 148.

[58] Davidson, *The Theology of the Old Testament,* 126.

Apart from spirit of human being and Spirit of God, spirit also signifies evil spirit where particular descriptions are attached to it. In this case the noun spirit is qualified by the epithet "evil" ([r),[59] or where a more particular description, such as "spirit of harlotry" (Hos. 4:12; 5:4), of jealousy (Num. 5:14), etc., characterizes the spiritual force as destructive. We also find "evil spirit of God;" and "evil spirit from God" (I Sam 19:9). Yahweh can indeed send these (evil) powers; yet they retain a certain independence of action (Judg. 9:23; II Kings 19:7 Cf. Isa. 29:10; 37:7). In spite of the fact that the Old Testament did not achieve a well-developed concept of demonic, the independence of evil power is mentioned explicitly.[60] The Old Testament view of evil spirit is characterized by the fact that the evil spiritual power is subordinated to the punishing God, and does not appear as an unpredictable demonic being, operating independently.

1.5. Spirit of Human being and the Spirit of God

One of the significant characteristics of spirit is that it is used for both human and for God. Consequently, it is hard to define whether it implies spirit of human being or the Spirit of God in some instances. Moreover, God's spirit and human's spirit are not sharply distinct from each other. God forms spirit in human beings (Zech. 12:1); it returns to God at death (Eccl. 12:7). Human's spirit is not something that he/she possesses simply by him/herself; it is a gift from God and depends continually on God (cf. Ps. 51:10). The vital power that comes from God is at the same time the breath or vital power by which all creatures live. This is depicted in Psalm 104:29-30 in which God's spirit is portrayed as the human life's breathe:

> When you hide your face, they are dismayed; when you take away their spirit, they die and return to their dust. When you send forth your spirit they are created; and you renew the face of the ground.

[59] Cf. I Sam. 16:14f; 18:10; 19:9; Judg. 9:23.

[60] Eichrodt finds parallel feature in Babylonia where the good wind has as its counterpart the evil wind, which brings sickness and is personified as a demon. See detailed discussion in Eichrodt, *Theology of the Old Testament* II, 55.

Here, their spirit (29) and your spirit (30) represent a transition that the spirit as the vital energy of God is passed to his creatures. The passage speaks simultaneously of their vital energy, the spirit of all living creatures. In v. 30 we see that the Spirit of God is the actual creative power, which creates and fills what would otherwise be lifeless (dust). Dorfel asserts that most of the Old Testament texts, which deal with human or divine spirit, depict God and humanity in such a dynamic relationship.[61] All life, whether in human or in lower creatures or in the world is an effect of the Spirit of God. All qualities of human abilities, strength, skills, wisdom, etc., are the gifts of God's spirit (cf. Exod. 28:3; 35:31, 34). Here, the divine and the human interact with one another in such a way that it is impossible to distinguish the artist's natural ability from what he experiences as given from beyond himself. Heron argues that spirit even as applied to man (sic) has an implicit reference to God as man's (sic) creator and sustainer.[62] Therefore, spirit refers both to God and to human life in its dependence upon God. Thus, spirit of human being is the life-giving force in human, which is also the life-giving effect of the Spirit of God.

1.6. The Spirit of God in the Old Testament

Theologically, in the Old Testament the most significant usage of spirit involves its representation of the metaphysical or numinous, specifically "the Spirit of God/the Lord." As pointed out in the above, spirit is used in various dimensions as wind, breath, spirit, etc. It is not always possible to distinguish theological from secular usage of the spirit. Horn notes that it is reasonable to associate spirit with God in the view of the wind's immateriality on the one hand, and its palpable power on the other.[63] The number of occurrence in

---

[61] Donata Dorfel, "The Divine Breathing: An Intercultural Investigation of the Holy Spirit," in *Challenges and Responses: Church's Ministry in the Third Millennium: Implications for Theological Education*, edited by Gnana Robinson (Bangalore: ATC, 2000), 332.

[62] Alasdair I. C. Heron, *The Holy Spirit* (Philadelphia: The Westminster Press, 1983), 7.

[63] F.W. Horn, "Holy Spirit," *ABD* Vol. 3, translated by Dietlinde E. Elliot, edited by Noel Freedman et al., (New York: Doubleday, 1992), 262.

the Old Testament is not easy to ascertain as different phrases are employed to represent the Spirit of God. Besides this, the subject matter and contexts of biblical texts determine the meaning of spirit and could signify both spirit in human or the Spirit of God. Roughly speaking the term spirit is employed to mean Spirit of God in the Old Testament nearly hundred times.[64] In English Bible the word "Spirit" is mainly employed to refer to the Spirit of God. According to Vriezen, It is either in the form of Spirit Elohim or Spirit Elohim or occasionally as the spirit, that the dynamic character (of God) is emphasized strongly, too, widely in different ways: as an external force or as a strong inward activity.[65] The Spirit of God may manifest itself as a violent storm of wind, but also as a seething power inspiring people and prompting them to perform tremendous deeds or as a power that overwhelms the entire emotional life of human. Therefore, the Spirit of God is God's exercising power, communicating, or operating in different dimensions. Eichrodt broadly describes the Spirit of God in the Old Testament as: (1) The principle of life (2) the instrument of the salvation history (3) the consummating power of new age, and (4) the power behind the life of the people of God.[66] The meaning and function of the Spirit of God could be traced along the development of theological understanding in the Old Testament period.

1.7. Spirit of Yahweh and Spirit of Elohim

When the Spirit of God is emphasized in biblical passages, two distinct expressions for God namely *Yahweh* and *Elohim* have been utilized with which the term spirit is associated. The usage includes expressions of spirit with Yahweh or Elohim either as a phase "Spirit Elohim/*Elohim*" or " spirit " "*the spirit*" or spirit with suffixes where the name of God in the context of the passage is Yahweh/Elohim.

[64] According to Brown, Driver and Briggs Spirit of God is found 94 times in the entire Old Testament while it is absent in Deuteronomy, Jeremiah or in any Deuteronomic writings. See *Lexicon*, 925. For detailed study on this matter see the Spirit of Yahweh and Spirit Elohim in the following discussion.

[65] Vriezen, *An Outline of Old Testament Theology*, 212.

[66] See more discussion on the subject in *Theology of the Old Testament* II, 46-68.

The number of occurrence and distribution of each of the term may be summarized as follows:[67]

1.7.1. Spirit of Yahweh

(a) Spirit of Yahweh: Judges - 7 times, I & II Samuel – 5, I & II Kings – 4, Isaiah – 6, Ezekiel – 2, Micah – 2, and II Chronicles – 2 = 27 times.[68]
(b) *My spirit*: Genesis – 1, Isaiah – 4 times, Ezekiel – 3, Joel – 2, Hagai – 1, Zechariah – 2 = 13times.[69]
(c) *His spirit*: Numbers – 1, Isaiah – 3, Zechariah – 1 = 5 times.[70]
(d) *Your spirit*: Psalm – 3 times = 3.[71]
(e) *Spirit*: Numbers – 1, I & II Kings – 3, I & II Chronicles – 3, Isaiah – 1, Ezekiel – 6 = 14 times.[72]
(f) *The spirit*: Numbers – 3, I Kings – 1, II Chronicles – 1, Hosea – 1 = 6 times.[73]
(g) *Holy spirit*: Psalm - 1, Isaiah – 2 times.[74]

The total number of occurrence of Spirit of Yahweh in the entire Old Testament therefore is 71.

---

[67] For this survey consult Albertz and Westermann, "רוח," *TLOT*, 1212-1213. See also Kohler & Baumgartner, "רוח," *HALOT*, 1200-1201.

[68] See Judges. 3:10; 6:34; 11:29; 13:25; 14:6; 14:19; 15:14; I Sam. 10:6; 16:13, 14; 19:9; II Sam. 23:2; I Kings 18:12; 22:24; II Kings 2:16; Isa. 11:2; 40:7, 13; 59:19; 61: 1; 63:14.

[69] See Gen. 6:3; Isa. 30:1; 42:1; 44:3; 59:21; Ezek. 36:27; 37:14; 39:29; Joel 3;1, 2; Hag. 2:5; Zech. 4:6; 6;8.

[70] See Num. 11:29; Isa. 30:28; 34:16; 48:16; Zech. 7:12.

[71] See Pss. 104:30; 139:7; 143:10.

[72] See Num. 27:18; I Kings 22:22, 23; II Kings 2:15; I Chro. 12:19; II Chro. 18:21, 22; Isa. 31:3; Ezek. 2:2; 3:12, 14, 24; 11:1; 43:5.

[73] See Num. 11:17, 25, 26, I Kings 22:21; II Chro. 18:10; Hos. 9:7.

[74] Ps. 51:13; Isa. 63:10, 11.

1.7.2. Spirit of Elohim

(a) Spirit of Elohim*:* Genesis – 2 times, Exodus – 2, Numbers – 1, I Samuel – 8, Ezekiel – 1 = 14 times.[75]

(b) *Spirit of Elohin* = 5 [76] (c) *Spirit of El:* Job 33:4 – 1, (d) *Spirit of Eloah:* Job 27:3 – 1, (e) *Spirit*: Job 32:8, Ezekiel 11: 24 = 2, Your *spirit* – Nehemiah 9:20, 30 = 2 times.[77]

The total number of occurrence of Spirit of Elohim in the Old Testament therefore is 25.

Looking at the occurrences and distribution one can assume that both Spirit of Yahweh and Spirit of Elohim are used interchangeably in some cases.[78] However, it is clearly shown that Spirit of Yahweh is more popularly used in the entire Old Testament. In general principle, there is no distinction as such in the meaning of Spirit of Yahweh and Spirit of Elohim.[79] However, at certain points, we may observe some distinctions in the use of the divine names in relation to the Spirit of God. Probably the best example for the distinction is seen in the case of the choice of David and rejection of Saul as found in I Sam. 16:14 –16. According to this text, "the Spirit of Yahweh had departed from Saul, and an evil spirit from Yahweh terrified him."[80] Henceforward we get the phrase "Spirit of Elohim" and "an evil Spirit of Elohim" used of Saul and his servants. The writers in this narrative seem to have been guided by two fixed principles: They were determined to retain the phrase "Spirit of Yahweh" with the

---

[75] See Gen. 1:2; 41:38; Exod. 31:3; 35:31; Num. 24:2; I Sam. 10:10; 11:6: 16: 15, 16, 23; 18:10; 19:20, 23; Ezek. 11:24(b).

[76] This is an Aramaic term equivalent to Elohim. See Dan. 4: 5, 6, 16; 5:11, 14.

[77] In these passages *ruah* is not attached to *Elohim* but used in the context where *Elohim* is used as the name of God in the passage.

[78] According to Snaith, in passages such as Num. 24:2, Zech. 7:12, II Chro. 15:1, 20:14; 24:20 we have application of "*Ruah Elohim*" and "*Ruah Yahweh*" without any change of meaning. See Snaith, *Distinctive Ideas of the Old Testament*, 154.

[79] Davidson, *The Theology of the Old Testament*, 125.

[80] It is interesting to note that the MT renders that "an evil *ruah* from Yahweh (Adonai)" was evil upon Saul, avoiding that the *ruah* (or *ruah Yahweh*) was evil. (See I Sam. 16:14ff). Here in this case, the good *ruah* is *ruah* Yahweh and the evil *ruah* is not in connection with Yahweh as the good *ruah*, though causally with him.

king whom God had chosen whereas the "Spirit Elohim" was evil, doubtless intending Elohim to be understood in the profane sense.

This is also in the case of a foreign prophet Balaam where the incoming of the Spirit of Elohim resulted into the experience of a trance (Num. 24: 2f.). The use of the Spirit of Yahweh is found primarily in the case of God enabling Israelite leaders.[81] Thus, the Spirit of Yahweh is the working might of Yahweh, as it served to deliver Israel, Yahweh's covenant-people, in particular. Spirit of Elohim in general appears to denote the marvelous, divinely imported power.[82] Hoyle argues that Spirit of Elohim calls attention to the soteriological purpose whereas Spirit of Elohim to the supersensible case.[83] We may conclude that the two phrases "Spirit of Yahweh" and "Spirit of Elohim" both signify the divine power, life giving power of God. However, Spirit of Yahweh is the working might of God as saviour and sustainer, and Spirit of Elohim is employed specifically to denote the marvelous, supersensible nature of God.

1.8. Conceptual Development of the Spirit of God in the Old Testament – A Brief Survey

The development of religious thought in Israel may also bring a conceptual development concerning God's spirit. Scott believes that the conception of the Spirit of God had found its place in Hebrew thought before the religion of Yahweh had emerged, or at least before it had arisen above the level of nature worship.[84] In the early days, the thought of the Spirit of God may not have anything essentially ethical or religious in their content. But this idea has undergone changes. For example, by the time of prophets of the Exile, the idea of the Spirit (Spirit of God) is ethicized and spiritualized (Cf. Ezek. 11:19; 36:26). According to Power, the concept of the Spirit of God

[81] See Judges. 3:10; 6:34; 11:29; 13:25; 14:6; 14:19; 15:14; I Sam. 10:6; 16:13, 14; 19:9; II Sam. 23:2; I Kings 18:12; 22:24; II Kings 2:16; Isa. 11:2; 40:7, 13; 59:19; 61: 1; 63:14.

[82] Example could be drawn from the case of Saul and Balaam. See I Sam 16:14ff; Num. 24:2f.

[83] R. Birch Hoyle, "Spirit of God," *Encyclopaedia*, 780.

[84] E.F. Scott, *The Spirit in the New Testament* (New York: George H. Doran Company, 1923), 14.

underwent changes in harmony with a developing understanding of God's nature and of his ways with men (sic).[85] Therefore, we will trace the development of the concept of Spirit of God in the Old Testament until the exilic age in the following.

1.8.1. The Spirit of God in Pre-Monarchic Period

In the earliest period of Old Testament literature the Spirit of God is presented in a materialistic fashion. Spirit is the divine essence as contrasted with human flesh (Gen. 6: 3).[86] Materially regarded is the spirit (of God) that is transferred from Moses to the seventy elders enabling them to prophesy (Num. 11:16-30 cf. II Kings 2:9). The Spirit of God in pre-monarchic period had a firm place in two contexts: in the charismatic leadership and ecstatic prophecy. In both contexts, spirit is a dynamically explosive force that overcomes a person and equips one for special acts of brief period.[87] However, spirit according to the Old Testament is the dynamic power of God. Thus the Spirit of God is upon Joseph so that he could interpret dreams (Gen. 41:38).[88] The J account of Moses' story is connected with both prophecy and ecstatic behaviour as The Spirit upon Moses was transferred to seventy (Num. 11:17-25). The same is true to the role of the Spirit Elohim upon Balaam whose influence is seen as ecstatic and prophetic in nature (Num. 24:2ff; 15).[89] The charismatic leadership of the Judges was associated with the endowment of

---

[85] Cyril H. Power, *The Biblical Concept of Power* (London: The Epworth Press, 1963), 27.

[86] The Text is considered to be a work of a Jehovist.

[87] According to Ancient Hebrew and Arab thoughts, those phenomenon of human personality that could not be explained were considered to be affected by an invasive spirit. See H. Wheeler Robinson, *The Religious Ideas of the Old Testament* (London: Gerald Duckworth & Co. Ltd., 1956), 110.

[88] According to Edmond Jacob, Apart from the figure of Joseph, the *ruah* Yahweh does not figure in the patriarchal narratives, nor in the those parts of the Pentateuch that deal with the laws (except in the data concerning the building of the tabernacle). *An Outline of Old Testament Theology*, 213.

[89] The text is attributed to the JE narratives. See discussion in Werner H. Schmidt, *Old Testament Introduction*, translated by Matthew J. O'Connell (Bandra, Bombay: St. Paul Publication, 1992), 99.

the Spirit of God. However, the endowment of the spirit is not of permanent, but of an abnormal communication of power from time to time.[90] There are eleven references to the Spirit of God coming upon the Judges (including Saul).[91] In all the cases the spirit (of God) enables the person in question to perform extraordinary deeds; to conquer enemies, etc.[92] However, the spirit that we find in operation among the judges is a kind of violent force which takes possession of specific persons and leads them to action in accordance with the demand of the situation.[93]

Thus, the role of Spirit of God is significantly seen in Deuteronomic preface with a programmatic section in which the schema of "apostasy-judgment-lament-deliverance" (Judg. 2:11-16) is characteristically transformed with the work of the Spirit Elohim.[94] The spirit animates the prophets in the pre-monarchic period and he who comes into contact with them is a willy-nilly so infected to become another man (I Sam. 10:6). We find the Spirit of God upon individual such as Samuel and also upon a company of prophets (I Sam 10:5-10). Ecstatic activity of the spirit can be seen in certain instances, where it is mostly associated with Elohim. However, the spirit of ecstatic prophecy is limited with regard to time and is marginal phenomenon in the Old Testament.[95] Thus, the Spirit of God in the period prior to monarchy was characteristically a dynamic force operated in at least two significant realms: in the realm of charismatic leadership and ecstatic prophecy. It is mainly temporary and individualistic in character.

---

[90] Sigmund Mowinckel, *He that Cometh*, translated by G.W. Anderson (New York: Abandon Press, 1954), 58.

[91] See Judges 3:10; 6:34; 11:29; 13:25; 14:6; 14:19; 16:14; and I Sam. 11:6.

[92] Thus Guillet claims that the *ruah* of God in the Old Testament is the source of the national community. Cited by Edmond Jacob, *An Outline of Old Testament Theology*, 124.

[93] Helmer Ringgren, *Israelite Religion*, translated by David Green (London: SPCK, 1966), 93.

[94] Albertz and Westermann, "*ruah*," *TLOT*, 1214.

[95] See discussion in John Samuel Raj, "Spirit and Kingship in the Old Testament," 22.

1.8.2. The Spirit of God in Monarchic Period

The transition from charismatic leadership to kingship changes the perception of the Spirit of God. The dynamic aspect gives way to a static understanding of spirit as related to office. The transition can be correctly located in I Sam 16:13f. with the transition of permanent office of David's monarchy. Thus, the Spirit Elohim becomes constant. The Spirit of God is bestowed and rests upon the blessed one (II Kings 2:15) who is thus filled with the Spirit of God (Deut 34:9). It no longer comes spontaneously but is linked to rites of anointing. The rites of anointing (I Sam. 16:13f.) as well as the laying of hands (Deut. 34:10) symbolize the change of perception. The gift of spirit and blessing become related concepts. Westermann observes that the narrative of I-II Kings consistently refers to the Spirit of God only in the context of royal accession or rule, never as an indication of special deeds or words.[96] Though it cannot always be determined with certainty whether this static understanding of spirit (of God) has been introduced retroactively from a later time, the notion is clearly present in the expectation of the messiah king (Cf. Isa. 11:2; Cf. 42:1; 61:1). Operation of the Spirit of God is seen in the narratives of kings of Israel, particularly Saul and David. We find eleven references where Saul is associated with the Spirit of God.[97] We have to notice that the Spirit (Spirit of God) left him only after the Lord rejected him. Moreover, once the Spirit left him, an evil spirit began to visit him in its place.[98]

There are two passages where the Spirit of God is associated with David. The first is in I Sam 16:3 where Samuel anointed David, which says, "…and the Spirit Elohim came mightily upon David from that day forward" This anointing was symbolic of the special

---

[96] Cited by F.W. Horn, "Holy Spirit," *ABD* Vol. 3, edited by David Noel Freedman et al., (New York: Doubleday, 1992), 263.

[97] In four instances it is the prophetic *ruah* that is referred to (I Sam. 10:6, 10; 19:20, 23). In I Sam. 11:6, the charismatic spirit comes upon Saul; in the other six instances (I Sam. 16:14, 15, 16, 23, 18:10; 19:9) it is the evil spirit from the Lord that rushed upon or torments Saul.

[98] See detailed study in Wilhelm Hertzberg, *I & II Samuel: A Commentary* (Philadelphia: The Westminster Press, 1964), 140-141.

endowment which the king receives in virtue of his office.[99] The second reference is found in II Sam. 23:1(b)-2. This is characterized by the style and thought of wisdom poetry where there is a description of the right kind of a king, who reigns in righteousness.[100] During monarchy there was another element namely the power of רוח רע (spirit of evil). Thus an evil spirit from God tortured Saul (I Sam. 16:14). The spirit in some instances are qualified by the epithet "evil" (I Sam. 16:14f; Cf. Judg. 9:23) or where a more particular description such as, spirit of harlotry (Hos. 4:12; 5:4), etc., characterize the spiritual force as destructive. The spirit of evil in the Old Testament is under the control of God, and is not appeared as a demonic being, operating independently.[101] God is thus said to have sent spirit of lying (II Kings 22:19-23). Evil spirit will be called evil Spirit of God because the Israelites attribute everything to God as the first cause.[102] We do not find any reference on the Old Testament indicating the Spirit of God with succeeding kings until the period of classical prophets.

1.8.3. The Spirit of God in Pre-exilic Classical Prophets

It was the task of the great prophets to develop that conception of Yahweh as a righteous God, which had always lain at the heart of Hebrew religion. From the prophets prior to the classical prophetic period, they took over the belief in the Spirit of God as the source of all that is extraordinary in human life. However, they bring it into harmony with their new conception of God. Even though the idea of the Spirit of God is not foreign to the activity of the great prophets of the pre-exilic age, classical prophets normally never speak of the possession of the Spirit of God in order to justify or authenticate their vision.[103]

---

[99] William McKane, *I & II Samuel: Introductory and Commentary* (London: SCM Press Ltd., 1963), 71.

[100] Samuel Raj, "Spirit and Kingship in the Old Testament," 31f.

[101] See Eichrodt, *Old Testament Theology* II, 55.

[102] A.M. Henry, *The Holy Spirit* (London: Burns & Oates, 1960), 23.

[103] Edmond Jacob, *Theology of the Old Testament*, 125.

According to Mowinckel the prophet's hesitation about the Spirit may have been due to conflicts with false prophets who boasted their possession of spirit.[104] The breaking away from the traditional idea of prophecy must have been deliberate, and was most probably due to the very fact that the Spirit (spirit) and prophetic madness were so closely connected in the popular mind (cf. Hosea 9:7). There seems to appear a shift from religious and ethical neutrality to teleological will and work of personal divine power.[105] Jepsen believes that the concept had been changed by social status of the prophets who were professional prophets as originated from professional order of Canaanite, consisting of men (sic) possessed by the Spirit of God, and distinct from both the soothsayer and seer or from ecstatic.[106] This is a probable cause for the shift in the understanding. Thus, for the prophets it is not the spirit but the "word" that which qualifies them for their ministry. However, the "word" presupposes the spirit, the creative breath of life, and for the prophets there was such evidence of this that they thought it unnecessary to state it explicitly.[107]

While pre-exilic classical prophets did not claim their mission as wrought by the Spirit of God, they do not refuse to be called "men (sic) of the spirit" among the people (Cf. Mic. 3:8). When Isaiah says of the Egyptians, "their horses are flesh and not spirit" (31:3), he seems to conceive of the spirit as the wisdom and power of God.[108] For the prophets the spirit sent forth from God partakes the higher quality of God as righteous and sovereign God. The Spirit of God is also portrayed as the bearer of divine judgment (Isa. 32:15). In this sense the Spirit of God is seen almost metaphysically, as the principle of the divine nature, as the equivalent of deity itself.[109] The ethical idea is indeed not directly emphasized; however, the Spirit of God will

---

[104] Sigmund Mowinckel, "The Spirit and the Word in the Pre-Exilic Reforming Prophets," *JBL* 53 (October, 1934): 207. According to Jeremiah the *ruah* of the prophets is nothing but only "wind" (Cf. Jer. 5:13).

[105] Baumgartel, "Spirit in the Old Testament," *TDOT*, 367.

[106] Cited by H. Wheeler Robinson, *Inspiration and Revelation in the Old Testament* (Oxford: Clarendon Press, 1946), 177.

[107] Edmond Jacob, *Theology of the Old Testament*, 125.

[108] Wonsuk Ma, "The Spirit (*ruah*) of God in Isaiah 1-39," 589.

[109] R. Birch Hoyle, "Spirit of God," *Encyclopaedia*, 787.

be upon a new (messiah) king so that he may establish justice (Isa.11: 2-4). The Spirit of God for pre-exilic classical prophets is associated not only with charismatic leadership and prophetic inspiration. It is the principle of divine nature with qualities of power. It is also the dynamic force through which divine judgment is established on earth.

1.8.4. The Spirit of God in Wisdom and Poetry

Wisdom and Poetic literature are considered to be written or compiled through a long period of time. Their original contents are considered to have come from the period before the exilic age.[110] The most important theme connected with the Spirit of God in Wisdom and Poetic literature is creation and maintenance of life. This is mainly found in association of spirit and *n^eshama* with giving and preserving of life.[111] Thus, "the Spirit of God has made me, and the *n^eshama* of the Almighty gives me life (Job 33:4 Cf. 34: 14-15). The creative activity of the Spirit of God is made explicit in Job 26:12-13 which says, "... by his spirit the heavens were made fair." Psalm 33:6 also alludes the activity of the spirit that "By the word of the Lord the heavens were made, and all their hosts by the spirit of his mouth."[112] Parallel reference is seen in the creation narrative of the Priestly writing[113] in

[110] While the final forms of Wisdom and Poetic literature are considered to be late, possibly, post exilic compilation. It is believed that they are originally written in the early period, prior to the exile. See chronological dates for Wisdom and Poetic literature of the Old Testament calculated by Robert H. Pfeifer, in *Introduction to the Old Testament* (New York: Harper & Row Publishers, 1948), 21-23.

[111] Heron, *The Holy Spirit*, 10.

[112] In Wisdom and Poetry we see theological development in the conception of creation by mere divine fiat. *Ruah* is coupled with *dabar* (word) and now means "the breath of speech rather than the breath of life" In this case; no distinct role is ascribed to the *ruah* and *dabar*. See more detail in Heron, *The Holy Spirit*, 11.

[113] Certain narratives in the Pentateuch are assigned to have come from the priestly writer/writers which are assigned to be written by the time of exile, or in the early post-exilic period. This is advocated by what is called Wellhausen hypothesis. See more detail in Werner H, Schmidt, *Old Testament Introduction*, 111-114. See also Julius Wellhausen, *Prolegomena to the History of Ancient Israel* (New York: The Meridian Books, 1956).

Gen 1:2c where the Spirit Elohim was hovering over the chaos in the time of creation.[114]

Ethical attributes are also assigned to the Spirit; it is called, good (Ps. 143:10 cf. Neh. 9:20), and thrice, holy (Ps. 51: 13; Isa. 63:10, 11). It is likely that the term "holy" is employed of the spirit and so the phrase "holy Spirit" indicates a principle which is both pure and inviolable.[115] The Spirit of God is described as the power behind the life of the people of God (Ps. 51:11). The wisdom schools are now open to the new assurance of Spirit's guidance in the congregation. Elihu can dispute authoritatively even with the old men in certainty that he is enlightened by the Spirit (Job 32:8ff., 18 cf. Dan. 4:5, 15; 5:11f.). It is the Spirit in a mortal, the breath of the Almighty that makes for understanding (Job 32:8). As Eichrodt affirms: "For the sage, it is the breath (spirit) of God that gives men (sic) understanding."[116] Turner's asserts that the pneumatology of wisdom and poetry holds that all authentic wisdom/understanding, creative work, art and culture, can be understood as manifestations of the spirit (spirit) of life that glorify God.[117] Thus, the Spirit of God in Wisdom and poetry is the creative and dynamic force of God, which is the source of all life and wisdom.

1.9. Summary

The foregoing studies have shown that the term רוח (spirit) primarily signifies a movement of air in the form of breath or wind, which however could also be a "spirit" in an anthropological and religious sphere. The cognate terms such as *n^e^shama* and *nephes* denote breath of life and life itself in the body respectively. The distinction of spirit

[114] There is a debate whether the *ruah* in Gen. 1:2c refers to the deity or the substance out of which Elohim creates the universe. See the debate in Michael DeRoche, "The Spirit Elohim in Gen. 1:2c: Creator or Chaos?," *Biblical and Other Studies in Memory of Peter C. Craigie*, edited by Lyle Eslinger & Glen Taylor (Sheffield: JSOT Press, 1988), 303-318.

[115] R. Birch Hoyle, "Spirit of God," *Encyclopaedia*, 788.

[116] Eichrodt, *Theology of the Old Testament* II, 63. Cf. Pv. 1:7; 9:10; 14:27; Ps. 143:10.

[117] M. Turner, "Spiritual Gifts," *New Dictionary of Biblical Theology*, edited by T.D. Alexander, et. al., (Leicester, England: InterVarsity Press, 2000), 791.

could be explained by the fact that *ruah* is the life-giving dynamic power behind the breath of human and personhood of an individual. *Ruah* as wind as a dynamic force and breath as a life-giving force are under the control and direction of God. *Ruah* as feeling and will are ramifications of the entire human personhood and are considered to be endowed by the power of God. One of the most significant usages of *ruah* is to be found in the theological realm. This is represented as "spirit" of human and of God. It is extremely difficult to distinguish between the spirit of human and Spirit of God in certain passages of the Old Testament. One could have assumed that the spirit of human being in any case is dependent on the life-giving power of God, known as the Spirit of God. The two titles for the Spirit of God namely, Spirit Elohim and Spirit Elohim are used interchangeably in most of the cases. However, they are different that the Spirit Elohim mainly refers to the salvific working power of God, and Spirit Elohim, the marvelous activity of God.

Along with the development of religious understanding in Israel, the Old Testament concept of the Spirit of God had also been developed in course of time. In the earliest stage of Israelite's history, the significant effect of Spirit of God was seen in the activity of charismatic leaders and ecstatic prophecy. When Monarchy emerged, the Spirit of God is conceived of as equipment of royal accession as a special endowment to become king. Pre-exilic classical prophets used the phrase "Spirit of God" with reservations. However, the Spirit of God signifies the principle of divine nature, as the equivalent of deity itself. Wisdom and Poetic literature depicts the Spirit of God as the life-giving and creative power of the divine, which is a source of all life and wisdom. We now observe a conceptual development of the Spirit of God in the Old Testament. It is in the exilic age that new developments of religious thought in general and the understanding of the Spirit of God in particular had been witnessed in ancient Israel. This will be dealt with in the forthcoming chapters.

Chapter 2

Historical Situations of the Exilic Age and Prophetic Responses

2.1. Introduction

The sixth century BCE has been often called a "creative age" as it was the period in which important events took place in a world-scale.[118] The period had significant landmark for the Israelites since it was the period of disaster as Judean kingdom collapsed with the subsequent tragic experience of the exile. Life in the exiles was not normal to the people, as they had been living in the unexpected life-situations. The period is not only epoch making in terms of tragedy but a period of new beginning as well. Great prophets appeared within the suffering communities whose response to the exiles formed profound theological literature of the Old Testament. Thus, chapter sketches

[118] The century is characterized by the rise of Confucianism, Zoroastrianism, and Buddhism in Asia; and it is also a century of great prophets of the Old Testament and many other literatures in West Asia. See more detail in Peter R. Ackroyd, *Exile and Restoration: A Study of Hebrew Thought of the Sixth Century* (London: SCM Press Ltd., 1968), 7.

the historical situations of the Israelites in the exilic age and prophetic responses to the situations.

Exile is traditionally taken to cover the period between the years 597-539 BCE[119] where considerable number of people of Judah were exiled in Babylonia and Egypt. Even though there is not much opposition to the historicity of the exile, there is also a belief that not all the people were taken captives. Therefore, Hermann rightly points out that the study of the exilic period has not to be confined to the deported people alone, but also with the population who had remained behind Judah.[120] The exile is generally considered to culminate with the edict of Cyrus in 539 BCE.[121] Therefore, the study of the historical situations in the exilic age here focuses on the Jews in Babylon, Judah and in Egypt during the period between the first deportation of the people of Judah in 597 and the fall of Babylon (539). The second part deals with a brief survey of prophetic responses towards this situation, concentrating on the three exilic prophets: Jeremiah, Ezekiel, and Deutero-Isaiah.

2.2. Sources of Information

Sources of information for the discussion are both biblical and extra-biblical witnesses. First, the Old Testament accounts are primary sources. However, the accounts are scattered and are not well documented. The Deuteronomistic history, one of the historical sources, ends with the exile and touches lightly on further developments in Judah and in Babylon. The books of Chronicles

---

[119] In this discussion Exile is taken to mean the Babylonian exiles of the 6th century BCE. The Assyrian exiles of the 8th and 7th century would not be dealt with. While some scholars regard the exilic age as ranging between 587/586-539 (See Rainer Albertz, *A History of Israelite Religion in Old Testament Period Vol. II: From the Exile to the Maccabees* (Louisville, Kentucky: Westminster John Knox Press, 1994), 369), the researcher reads the year 597 BCE as a starting point of exilic age as it witnesses deportation of many people including king Jehoiakin with high officials.

[120] Siegfried Hermann, *A History of Israel in the Old Testament Times* (London: SCM Press Ltd., 1975), 289.

[121] Following the edict of Cyrus in 539, certain groups of people went (ready to go) up and rebuilt the house of the Lord in Jerusalem, and hence it is generally considered the end of the exile (Cf. Ezra 1:1-5).

end with the fall of Jerusalem and append the edict of Cyrus briefly. The other available Old Testament sources are scattered in prophets, and poetry. Secondly, we have a series of extra-biblical documents of different genres and tendencies about the reign of the last Babylonian king Nabonidus and the fall of Babylon. These documents chiefly comprise of the Babylonian Chronicle for the years 555-539.[122] There are also archaeological evidences, which attest the deportation to Egypt, which are found in Elephantine Papyri.[123] Archaeology of different sites in Palestine, [124] and certain ostraca found in different sites also contribute to the understanding of historical situations of the exilic age.[125] Other important sources for our study are the *Antiquities of the Jews* by Josephus[126] and the writings of Old Testament scholars.

2.3. The Fall of Jerusalem

With the help of biblical and extra-biblical sources we can project the history of Israel with the destruction of Jerusalem that resulted into exile in the sixth century BCE. I hereby briefly summarize the

[122] See James S. Pritchard (ed), *Ancient Near Eastern Texts Relating to the Old Testament (ANET),* translated by A. Leo Openheim (Princeton: Princeton Univ. Press, 1955), 305-307 (Hereafter *ANET*).

[123] Elephantine papyri are Aramaic documents belonging to the fifth century BCE found at Elephantine, in the river bank of Aswan, which have been termed "The Elephantine Papyri." See *ANET*, 222. See also discussion in Peter R. Ackroyd, *Israel Under Babylon and Persia*, (Great Britain: Oxford University Press, 1970), 279.

[124] The excavations at Debir, Lachish, and Beth-Shamesh (which are in the south and southeast part of Judah) reveal the intensity of the destruction and of the exile that these cities were completely annihilated at the time of Nebuchadnezzar. See more detail in Arvid S. Kapelrud, *Israel from the Earliest Times to the Birth of Christ,* translated by J.M. Moe (Oxford: Basil Blackwell, 1966), 105.

[125] Excavations at Nipur undertaken by Pennsylvania University help to understand the socio-economic condition of the exiles in Babylon. W.O.E. Oesterley, *A History of Israel,* Vol. II (Oxford: The Clarendon Press, 1939), 45.

[126] "The Antiquities of the Jews" was written by Josephus, a Jewish historian who lived in the first century CE in the Roman court as a client of the emperor. His work came in to existence by the time after the destruction of Jerusalem in 70 CE. See the Introduction in William Whiston (trans.) *The Works of Josephus: Complete and Unabridged* (United Sates: Hendrickson Publishers, 1987), ix. (Hereafter, *Works of Josephus*).

end of Judah and the exile so as to help us understand the historical situations in the exilic age. After the death of king Josiah (609), the Egyptians put his son Jehoahaz to the throne as a vassal king of Judah. But after three months reign, he was deposed and Jehoiachim, his elder brother was put to the throne by the same imperial ruler (Jer. 22:10-12). Following these events, Babylonia with its strong king Nebopalassar and his successor Nebuchadnezzar overpowered the Egyptian domination.[127]

Jehoiachin the other son of Josiah succeeded Jehoiachim in 598 BCE.[128] Nebuchadnezzar besieged Jerusalem in 597 BCE and took Jehoiachin to exile with other officials (II Kings 24:13-17). The newly enthroned king of Judah, Zedekiah continued to rebel against Babylonia which led to the greatest ever destruction of Jerusalem in 587 BCE.[129] The king was blinded and many people including high officials, priests, craftsmen, artisans and others were taken to Babylon.[130] Thus the glorious days of Judah were ended. However, life was continued in Babylonia as they were exiled in a foreign land until the edict of Cyrus in 539 BCE. It is also attested that life was continued in Judah during the period.[131] The exile was then caused by recurring deportations in the sixth century.

2.4. The First Deportation

On the 16th March 597 BCE Nebuchadnezzar captured the city of Judah and deported a number of people from Jerusalem. According to the Deuteronomic historian this deportation numbers as much

---

[127] The Egyptian power was humiliated at the famous war at Carchemis in 605 BCE. See *ANET,* 305ff.

[128] William L. Holladay, "The Years of Jeremiah's Preaching," *Interpretation* XXXVII/2 (April, 1983): 154.

[129] Josephus has two separate attacks in 587, which led the final destruction. See William Whiston (trans.) *The Works of Josephus: Complete and Unabridged* (United Sates: Hendrickson Publishers, 1987), ix.

[130] Cf. II Kings 25:12; II Chro. 36:20; Jer. 39:1-7.

[131] The excavations carried out by Kathleen Kenyon from 1961-1967 on the southeastern hill of Jerusalem reveal that the main hill of Jebusite and then Davidic city were still in occupation in the (early) 6th century. See the discussion in Peter R. Ackroyd, *Israel Under Babylonia and Persia*, 6.

as 10,000 deportees including king Jehoiachin (II Kings 24:14-15) and prophet Ezekiel (Ezek. 1:1-2). The Babylonian record gives no number of captivity. In Jeremiah 52:28 a rather smaller figure is recorded: 3023 people (not in the LXX). Josephus has two deportations.[132] Malamat reckons that the total number to be 10,000 men, which with their families, would mean about 30,000 actual deportees.[133] Coggin's comment in this regard is likely that it is possible to reconcile differences of the kind by supposing that different bases for counting were being used.[134]

2.5. The Second Deportation

The second deportation of the Jews was resulted by the fall of Jerusalem in 587 BCE. In this deportation, Zedekiah, the last king of Judah was blinded and brought to Babylonia with many other captives. II Chronicles reports that the king of the Chaldeans took into exile in Babylon those who had escaped from the sword (II Chro. 36:20). In the tabulations appended to the book of Jeremiah, these exiles on the occasion of the destruction of Jerusalem amounted to 832 persons (Jer. 52:29). Coggin believes that the Deuteronomistic historian suggests that the real communities of the deported people are those taken against their will.[135] The number and destinations of the second groups of captivity (587) is uncertain. Among the captives was prophet Jeremiah. But he was released (Jer. 4:1-4).

---

[132] *Woks of Josephus*, 272 & 273. The record numbers 3000 and 10832. The record of Josephus seems to be repetition since no other records are found in favour of it. Ackroyd believes that Josephus has here conflated the two figures taken from the two accounts on II Kings 24-25 and Jeremiah 52. See Peter R. Ackroyd, *Exile and Restoration* (London: SCM Press, 1968), 23.

[133] Cited by Peter R. Ackroyd, *Exile and Restoration*, 23.

[134] Richard J. Coggins, "The Exile History and Ideology," *The Expository Times* 110/12 (September, 1999): 389. The Deuteronomistic historian emphatically says that "With him (Zedekiah) went the last of the people remaining in the city, and those who deserted to the king of Babylon-all the rest of the population, leaving only the poorest people to be vinedressers and laborers" (II King 25: 11-12).

[135] Richard J. Coggins, "The Exile History and Ideology," 390.

2.6. The Third/Final Deportation

In addition to the deportations in 597 and 587 BCE an added list of exile is referred to in the book of Jeremiah, which numbers 745 persons (52:30). According to Jeremiah, Nebuzaradan the captain of the guard carried out the third deportation in the twenty-third year (of the reign of) Nebuchadnezzar, i.e., 583/582 BCE possibly as a retaliation of the assassination of Gedaliah. The unknown size of population dispersed and exiled to Egypt, following the assassination of Gedaliah and fear of Babylonian invasion (II Kings 25:22-26). The group set out for Egypt taking Jeremiah and his companion with them. They reached Tahpanhes, an Egyptian border fortress east of the Nile delta near Pelusim (Jer. 44:1). The existence of a Jewish military colony at Elephantine at the southern border of Egypt in the sixth and fifth centuries BCE is attested by excavated documents.[136]

2.7. The Exile

The Babylonian exile had been the subject of much recent discussion since some OT scholars have articulated doubt concerning its historicity. The Old Testament accounts are scattered and must be taken from a variety of literary works. The Chronicles does not speak of the exile at all. Deuteronomistic history ends with the fall of Jerusalem in 587, and only touches lightly on further developments in Judah (II Kings 25:22-30). Thus, C.C. Torrey questions whether there ever was an exile, claiming that the story was made up to justify the existence of Jews in Babylonia at a later period.[137] However, not many scholars followed Torrey's hypothesis. A Babylonian Court list, which mentions Jehoiachin and calls him "king of the land of Judah," testifies the existence of deported Jews with their exiled king Jehoiachin.[138] A record from a Babylonian business company

---

[136] Elephantine is a Greek name of the island of Yeb in the Nile, an island situated opposite to Syene (modern Assuan), which is on the riverbank. Aramaic documents belonging to the fifth century BCE have been found (in these sites) which have been termed "The Elephantine Papyri." See *ANET*, 222. See also discussion in Peter R. Ackroyd, *Israel Under Babylon and Persia*, 279.

[137] Cited by Richard J. Coggins "The Exile History and Ideology," 389.

[138] *ANET*, 308. Cf. II Kings 25:27-30.

at Nippur has also attested the existence of deported Jews.[139] Biblical records as well as Josephus support this thesis. Therefore, the historicity of the exile is generally accepted. It is not easy to provide the exact date when the exile ends, because not all the deported Jews returned home after the fall of Babylonia in 539. In this discussion we assume exile is scheduled to have begun in 597 BCE with the first deportation and ends with the edict of Cyrus in 539.

2.8. Historical Situations in the Exilic Age

The collapse of Judah and the subsequent deportations and the exile marked a decisive turning point on the historical life of the Israelite nation. It is not easy to determine precisely how many people were deported, since the records were not decisive. The historical situations of the exilic community in Babylonia, Judah, and Egypt will be discussed as follows:

2.8.1. In Babylonia

As stated in the foregoing study, a number of people were deported to Babylonia including kings and many officials of Judah in 597/587. The situation in Babylonia is difficult to describe with precision for lack of sufficient sources. Most of the commentators assume that the lot of the Jewish exiles in Babylonia was far from being a hard one. The historical situations of Babylonian exile may be summarized as follows:

2.8.1.1. Political Situation

There is very good reason to believe that Nebuchadnezzar's enlightened policy in regard to Palestine was similarly exhibited in his treatment of the exiles. He was a strong king who assailed further campaigns in the west after the destruction of Jerusalem.[140] But after his death in 562 BCE, Babylonian power rapidly declined. Awil

---

[139] See *ANET*, 221f. This record suggests that the Jews were also participated in the business affairs of the time. See detailed discussion in Peter R. Ackroyd, *Israel Under Babylon and Persia* (Great Britain: Oxford University Publications, 1970), 19ff.

[140] *ANET*, 305. Cf. *Works of Josephus*, 279f; Ezek 26&28, & Jer. 52:30.

Marduk ruled from 562-560 whose relation with king Jehoiachin is recorded in a Babylonian Court list.[141] The dispute of succession of the throne was continuing until its last king Nabonidus who came into power in 555 BCE, who had a strange character.[142]

The Babylonian empire came to an end in 539 BCE as Gobryas the commander of Cyrus overthrew it, and became under the Persian hands.[143] Cyrus the Persian king issued the edict, which allowed the Exiles to return home which resulted the return of 42,360 to Judah (Ezra 2:65 Cf. Neh.7: 67). There is not much information about the political activity of the Jews in Babylonia. However, a record of the Babylonian Court list reveals that king Jehaoiachin was released from prison and was given a royal status in Babylonia during the reign of Awil Merodach.[144] There is also reference to "Gatherings of the elders of Judah" in Babylonia (Ezek. 8:1; 14:1; 20:1), which may possibly indicate their ancient positions of leaders of different communities.[145] Therefore, the Jews in Exile might have a limited communal self-government.

2.8.1.2. Socio-Economic Situation

The early part of the book of Ezekiel and Jeremiah (even if contrary to the later tradition) show clearly that the exiles are not prisoners that they lived in several places, mainly in the river Chebar, perhaps river canal of Euphrates.[146] They lived in the locations in families (Ezra 2:59), or according to professional groups (Ezra. 8:17). Alongside

---

[141] *ANET*, 308. Cf. II Kings 25: 27-30.

[142] The policy of Nabonidus allowed the political organization to decay and fell out with the priests of the imperial god Marduk in Babylon that has been considered to be responsible for the weakening of the kingdom. See Martin Noth, *The History of Israel* (London: Adam & Charles Black, 1960), 300f.

[143] Hermann, *A History of Israel*, 295.

[144] See the reference in II Kings 25:27-30. Cf. Jeremiah 52:31-34.

[145] Oesterley, *A History of Israel* Vol. II, 45.

[146] The Murashu Tablets were found in Nippur, which attest that there were a number of Judahites in the settlements. Cited by Rainer Albertz, in *A History of Israelite Religion in the Old Testament Period, Vol. II From the Exile to the Maccabees*, translated by John Bowden, (London: SCM Press Ltd., 1994), 599. Cf. Ezek. 1:1, 3, and *ANET*, 221f.

priests and prophets, elders took over functions of leadership (Jer. 29:1; Ezek. 7:1; 14:1). It looks as though after some initial difficulties the socio-economic situation was by no means oppressive for the exiles of Judah. They were able to build houses, plant gardens and enjoy their products. They were able to marry and live normal lives (Jer. 29:5-7). They were legally fully integrated in Babylonia and got along quite normally in their business.[147] They could rise to higher positions in the service of high offices (Ezra 7:14; Neh. 7:44). The ability to exchange correspondence with Jeremiah or his superiors in Jerusalem indicates literacy and freedom (Jer. 29). While there are considerable supports for the socio-economic well-being of the people of Judah, there are also distress of the prophet(s) and times of laments which suggest oppressive nature of the Babylonia. The distress of Ezekiel (Ezek. 4:14) and that of the weight of disaster (Ezek. 37) denote the arduous treatment they received in the exile. The heartfelt cry of Psalms 137 suggests real sensitivity to its oppressiveness. Deutero Isaiah's announcement of joyful deliverance from the tyrant's hand portrays Cyrus as a liberator from oppressions of the Babylonian power (Isa. 45:1-7; 51:12-16). Martin Noth thus called the exiles a "compulsorily transplanted subject population."[148] In spite of favourable conditions in terms of socio-economic status, the exile means a social uprooting as they lost their land and their authentic social status.

2.8.1.3. Religious Situation

The religious policy of Babylonia in the earlier part of the exile seems favourable and tolerance. However, traces of change might be seen with Nabonidus, the last king of Babylonia.[149] For Pfeiffer the community in Babylonia was in fact a religious community free

---

[147] *ANET*, 221f. Business documents of the Murushu family in the second half of the fifth century found at Nipur, south east of Babylon recorded few Jewish names in relation to trade with men of other nationalities.

[148] Noth, *The History of Israel*, 296.

[149] Nabonidus was considered to impose religious intolerance as he patronized worship of "sin god" which is distinct from Babylonia's religion. See details in Ronal H. Sack, "Nabonidus," *Anchor Bible Dictionary* Vol. 4, edited by Noel Freedman et al., (New York: Doubleday, 1992), 975. Cf. Dan. 3.

from political entity and cultic centre.[150] There is little on which any conclusion can be based regarding worship in the exilic situation. Blenkinsopp's observation that there is a possibility that the deportees built their own temple at Casiphia, one of the centres of the diaspora is not proved.[151] Ackroyd assumes possible connection of "assembly of elders" by the Chebar, with worship.[152] There is no evidence that there were any organized local assemblies for worship and teaching in synagogues. However, one can safely say that the later synagogues which came to be scattered throughout the countries of the dispersion, arose in response to a need that was first experienced during the exile.[153]

Even though there are not sufficient sources, which define religious conditions of the exile, scholars are in the opinion that certain religious practices (like circumcision and observance of the Sabbath) received importance.[154] It is believed that the exile was a time of religious activity, a time of concentrated attention to Israel's religious heritage. Some of the editing of the prophetic and historical literature was done in this period by anonymous redactors (usually called the Deuteronomists). The final form of the Pentateuch came into existence with the works of the priestly writers.[155] In recent decades many Old Testament scholars observe the reshaping of Israel's faith during the exilic period, which resulted in the formation

---

[150] C.F. Pfeiffer, "History of the People of Israel" *ISBE* Vol. Two, edited by Geoffrey W Bromiley et. al., (Grand Rapids, Michigan: Eerdmans, 1988), 918.

[151] For Blenkinsopp, the presence of a certain Iddo (a priest) in Casiphia from which Ezra recruited cultic personal in the postexilic period advocates the thesis. See, Joseph Blenkinsopp, *A History of Prophecy in Israel* (revised and enlarged) (Kentucky: Westminster John Knox Press, 1996), 271. Cf. Ezra 8:15-20).

[152] Peter R. Ackroyd, *Exile and Restoration: A Study of Hebrew Thought of the Sixth Century* (London: SCM Press Ltd., 1968), 33f.

[153] Bernhard W. Anderson, *Understanding the Old Testament* (New Jersey: Prentice-Hall, Inc., 1957), 379.

[154] For a detailed discussion see H. Wheeler Robinson, *The Religious Ideas of the Old Testament* (London: Gerald Duckworth & Co. Ltd., 1956), 207. Also Ralph W. Klein, *Israel in Exile: A Theological Interpretation* (Philadelphia: Fortress Press, 1979).

[155] Anderson, *Understanding the Old Testament,* 380.

of profound literary works.[156] The rival Babylonian religion was a tribute to Israel's tenacity and vitality that the Mosaic faith not only survived this transition but also was immeasurably deepened and enriched thereby.[157] One has to conclude that in spite of lack of sufficient evidence for religious activities in the exiles of Babylonia, there would have been a certain kind of worship and Israel's profound religious literature including prophetic literature had emerged.

2.8.2. In Judah

Biblical records and archaeological evidences have attested the destruction of Jerusalem in the early part of the sixth century. However, the precise nature of destruction of Judah and the number of exiles could not be ascertained with precision. Archaeology of different sites of Palestine attests the continuing settlement of Judah in the sixth century BCE.[158] In spite of reports of large-scale devastation, texts of II Kings 25 and Jeremiah 52 have suggested that depopulation cannot have been so extensive. The historical situations in Judah may be described as follows:

2.8.2.1. Political Situation

After the fall of Jerusalem the country was put into the charge of a native official from Judah named Gedaliah who ruled from Mizpah, north of Jerusalem (Jer. 40-44; II Kings 25:22-26). Gedaliah formed

---

[156] For example Klein brings out six literary works as the outcome of the exile, such as Lamentations, selected Psalms, Deuteronomistic History, Priestly writings of the Pentateuch, prophets of Jeremiah, Ezekiel and Deutero-Isaiah. See Klein, *Israel in Exile*, 7. See also works such as Walter Brueggemann, *Hopeful Imagination: Prophetic Voices in Exile* (Philadelphia: Fortress Press, 1986), Peter R. Ackroyd, *Exile and Restoration*, and Albertz, *A History of Israelite Religion* Vol. II. Etc.

[157] Some scholars observe the religious policy of Marduk (the last king of Babylonia) as a threat to Jewish faith in exile that there arose hostility towards this policy in prophetic literature of the time and in the book of Daniel. (For example in Isaiah 13-14; 21; 45 and 47; Jeremiah 50 and 51, Dan. 4) See discussion in Siegfried Hermann, *A History of Israel*, 37. Cf. Peter R. Ackroyd, *Exile and Restoration*, 37.

[158] D.J. Wiseman notes that towns in the south (Negeb) and to the north of the border (Bethel) and in the Babylonian province of Samaria have been found undestroyed in this critical time. Cited by P.R. Ackroyd, *Exile and Restoration,* 22. Cf. Pfeiffer, "History of the People of Israel," 919.

a centre in Mizpah around which the Judeans who had not been taken into exile might gather.[159] But it seems that this was intended to be only a temporary expedient, and that Jerusalem soon became once more the centre of government.[160] The country suffered partition, the northern state becoming the Babylonian province and the rest of Judah suffered from the attacks of the population from the Ammonites, Moabite, Edom, Phoenicians, and Philistines.[161]

The rule of Gedaliah at Mizpah came to a violent end. Ishmael, a man of royal blood who was supported by the king of Ammon killed him. He took captive the others who had settled at Mizpah (Jer. 41:4-7). However, the forces of the loyal Johanan, the son of Kareah confronted Ishmael and the latter fled to the land of Ammonites, and his captives were freed (Cf. Jer. 41:7ff.). Johanan and his groups who were afraid of the intervention of the Babylonians fled to Egypt took with them prophet Jeremiah. Since the Babylonians did not impose its administration to the whole area, Judah could develop a limited degree of self-government on the basis of elders (Cf. Lam. 5:12). Thus, Judah's political entity was somewhat controlled by the Babylonians and confronted by neighbouring states. However, Judah enjoyed self-government to a certain period or to a certain extent.

2.8.2.2. Socio-Economic Situation

We may assume that Judah suffered famine and poverty at the immediate period of destruction. The consequent attacks from foreign nations and occasional confrontations of the Babylonian power would have worsened the socio-economic life of the people of Judah (Lam. 1:11; 2:12, 20; 4:4, 10). However, The rise of Gedaliah into power under the Babylonia led the inhabitants including refugees of the land drifted back to normalcy and they resumed agriculture (Jer. 40:10-12). Thus the land that has been devastated by the war

---

[159] The rule of Gedaliah is attested by an inscription found at Lachish (Tell-ed-dweir) inscribed, "to Gedaliah who is over the house" which probably refers to the same person as a ruler of the capital. See *ANET*, 322.

[160] Oesterley, *A History of Israel* II, 36.

[161] See references in Jer. 49:1-6 Cf. Ezek. 25:1-11; 35:1-15; Lam. 5:12-13; Amos 1:11f; Joel 4:6.

recovered economically.[162] Removal of officials, priests and landed citizens (probably partial) resulted a social revolution in Judah. This could have been affected by the rising to positions of greater influence of those who could be described as the "poor of the land" (*dallat ha ares*) (II Kings 25). The presumably propertyless members of the community, who became landholders under the Babylonian authority, occupied royal lands and perhaps also took over lands from other property-owners.[163] For the majority of those who were left in the land, the exile was Yahweh's judgment is the exploitation of the upper class and often even a *de facto* liberation from debt.[164] Thus, administration was partly in the hand of the inhabitants on the basis of elders. Due to constant threat from foreign nations and lack of strong administration, the socio-economic condition of Judah might have worsened.[165] Therefore, Judah at the time of exiles enjoyed some kind of socio-economic independence, which was however constantly checked and weakened by the intrusion of foreign nations.

2.8.2.3. Religious Situation

The worse effect of the catastrophe experienced by Judah in the 6th century may probably be its effect upon the worship of Yahweh. The temple was destroyed; sacred vessels were robbed (II Kings 25:9). It is often being assumed that the Ark too was destroyed.[166] Whether worship was done in Temple is uncertain. Jer 41:32 reports that worships were done in the temple in the period of Gedaliah. According to Jeremiah 41:5 even after the destruction of Jerusalem people came from Shechem, Shilloh, and Samaria possibly for pilgrimage to Jerusalem to make sacrifice to the house of Yahweh.[167]

---

[162] Albertz, *A History of Israelite Religion, Vol II.* 372.

[163] Ackroyd, *Exile and Restoration*, 23f.

[164] Albertz, *A History of Israelite Religion, Vol. II.* 372.

[165] For example the attempt of rebuilding Jerusalem walls was constantly disturbed by Samaritans at the beginning of return from exiles (Cf. Ezra 4:7-16).

[166] M. Haran believes that king Manasseh had already removed the Ark. See more details in Ackroyd, *Exile and Restoration*, 25.

[167] While sacrifice is mentioned, only cereal offering and incense are mentioned in Jeremiah. This could point to the fact that full sacrificial system could

Ackroyd argues that rebuilding of the temple in the later period was not apparently done in a disused site; and it would suggest an earlier revival.[168]

Some scholars propose that some of the Old Testament literatures such as Deuteronomistic History, Lamentations and fragments of prophetic messages were of Palestine origin in the exilic age.[169] If we look at the responses of prophets and laments, we also could draw a conclusion that worship of Yahweh had become prostituted and there is evidence of worship of alien cults including Tamuz and the sun deity (Ezek. 5:5-10; 8:9-18; 22:1-37; 33:27-29). It is against this background that we could understand the collection of liturgical laments that we call Lamentations which reflect the situations who are in the homeland.[170] Therefore, in spite of possible religious activities, religious condition in the homeland was corrupted.

2.8.3. In Egypt

Unlike Babylonian exile, the Egyptian exile did not happen as a result of compulsory deportation, but through voluntary emigration for fear of Babylonian reprisals after the murder of Gedaliah (II Kings 25:26). They settled in various places in lower and Upper Egypt (possibly at Migdol, Daphne and Memphis) (Jer. 44:1). The settlement suggests that the group sought and made its living above all as soldiers in Egyptian Service.[171] Whether the later Jewish military colony in Elephantine also goes back to this group of emigrants is uncertain, but it does bear witness to a similar social milieu.[172] We can see from

---

not be resumed, or this limited sacrifice was appropriate to the particular worship of lamentation. See Ackroyd, *Israel Under Babylonia and Persia*, 25.

[168] Ackroyd, *Exile and Restoration*, 29. Cf. Ezra 3.

[169] Jensen, D.J. Smart and Ralph W. Klein are some of the scholars. See Klein, *Israel in Exile*, 1-8. Also, Ackroyd, *Exile and Restoration*, 31.

[170] Edgar Jones, "Exile and Post Exilic Period: 587-175" *The Bible and History* (London Lutterworth Press, 1968), 125.

[171] See "Letters of the Jews in Elephantine" in *ANET*, 492.

[172] Aramaic documents belonging to the fifth century BCE have been found (in these sites) which have been termed "The Elephantine Papyri," See more detail in Peter R. Ackroyd, *Israel Under Babylon and Persia*, 279.

the texts which have survived from this colony that the Egyptian exiles became even more integrated socially into its host society. The Egyptian exiles were organized as worshiping community as they also had the temple of Yahweh, which was founded before 525 BCE, possibly still during the exile.[173] Thus, exilic community in Egypt formed a well-organized religious group.

2.9. Prophetic Responses to the Exiles

2.9.1. Who are Exilic Prophets?

Scholars are not of the same opinion in ascribing prophets of the exilic period. This is implied by a suggestion that in prophetic literature biographies of the prophets as well as their prophecies are represented along successive redactions and thus it is difficult to refer to the original authors' work.[174] For most of the scholars prophets of the exilic age include the three prophets: Jeremiah, Ezekiel and Deutero Isaiah[175] since the literature of these three prophets reflect upon the exile and that the prophets themselves shared the tragedy. Thus they shaped their literature to help people enter into exile, to be in exile and depart out of exile.[176] While some scholars include Jeremiah among the exilic prophets,[177] some others exclude him because his ministry was mainly seen in the pre-exilic period (627-

---

[173] Albertz, *The History of Israelite Religion II*, 374.

[174] Two theories are proposed to define the process of redactions in the literary collections: (1) the belief that the formation of the books has been the result of a process of continuous, and more or less unrelated, agglomeration of material, and (2) each of the great prophets gave rise to the organization of the body of disciples, who could then have been responsible for the preservation of the original prophet-master's sayings and for the addition of further prophecies to these. See detailed discussion in Ronald E. Clements, *Old Testament Prophecy: From Oracles to Canon* (Louisville, Kentucky: Westminster John Knox Press, 1996), 146ff.

[175] The role of Jeremiah and Ezekiel are recorded by Josephus where as Deutero-Isaiah is not mentioned. See *Works of Josephus*, 272ff.

[176] Brueggemann, *Hopeful Imagination*, 1.

[177] Thus Ackroyd, *Exile and Restoration*. Thomas M. Raitt, *A Theology of Exiles* (Philadelphia: Fortress Press, 1977), Ralph W. Klein, *Israel in Exile*, Brueggemann, *Hopeful Imagination.*, and others.

587).[178] Some others believe that the other prophet named Obadiah is also active in the period.[179] In this discussion, the researcher is not bringing out critical problems involved in the study of the exilic prophets;[180] rather we will come to the prophetic response to the exiles.

2.9.1.1. Jeremiah

Source critics are of the opinion that the book of Jeremiah is a compilation of different literary works.[181] For Nicholson, the book of Jeremiah has been reworked in order to be pertinent to the theological crisis of the exile, so that the book reflects the creative work of the generation.[182] In this discussion of Jeremiah's response we will take the literature as a composite literary unit by dating the response in the period just before and just after the destruction of Jerusalem in 587. Jeremiah was the first known prophet who actually experienced the disaster of 587. Born from a priestly family at Anathoth he received his call in the year 627/626 (Jer. 1:13f.), his prophetic activity spanned forty years (627-587).[183] He was one of the exilic prophets who shared the catastrophe of the sixth century BCE Israel.

---

[178] Thus excluded by Canon Sell in *Prophets of the Exile* (Madras: Diocesan Press, 1923). Also See "Religion of Exilic Period" by George Fohrer, *History of Israelite Religion*, translated by David E. Green (London: SPCK, 1972), 307ff., also Joseph Dheily, *The Prophets* (New York: Hawthorn Books, 1960), 29.

[179] Though considered to be prophesied after the fall of Jerusalem, the exact date of the book is still a matter of debate. See Robert R. Wilson, *Prophecy and Society in Ancient Israel* (Philadelphia: Fortress Press, 1980), 287.

[180] This will be dealt with in the next chapters where each prophet will be dealt with in more detail.

[181] The main argument is that the original work of Jeremiah and Baruch (A+B) are supplemented by a collection of sermons (C), which was compiled with another addition by a final redactor known as the Deuteronomist. See detailed discussion in Brueggemann, *To Pluck Up to Tear Down: A Commentary on the Book of Jeremiah 1-25* (Grand Rapids: Eerdmans, 1988), 7f.

[182] Ernest. W. Nicholson, *Preaching to Exiles* (Oxford: Basil Blackwell, 1970), 14.

[183] Anderson, *Understanding the Old Testament*, 326.

2.9.1.2. Ezekiel

Ezekiel is also a prophet who experienced the tragedy of the exile. He is a prophet-priest exiled in 597 along with king Jehoiakin and others. Von Rad believes that Ezekiel received his call in Babylon in the year 593, and he exercised his office from then on until about 571.[184] The authenticity of the book is a matter of debate.[185] G.B. Gray, however, affirms that no other book of the Old Testament is distinguished by such a decisive marks of unity of authorship and integrity than the book of Ezekiel.[186] It is agreeable when K. von Rabenau writes that in view of the similarity in form and content we must postulate a close interconnection between prophet and a redactor; perhaps direct relationship with a disciple.[187] Therefore, the book can be taken as a literary unit, which reflects the catastrophe of the sixth century, more suitably the exiles in Babylonia.

2.9.1.3. Deutero-Isaiah

Following Duhm's study on Isaiah, the book of Isaiah 40-55 has been considered the work of an unknown prophet in the late Babylonian period (550-540).[188] In spite of the debate about the above thesis,[189]

---

[184] G. von Rad, *The Message of the Prophets* (New York: Harper & Row, 1965), 189.

[185] One of the main arguments against the authorship of Ezekiel is the intimate knowledge of events taking place in Palestine in the first part of the book (1-24), which suggests a Palestinian author than an exiled prophet of Babylonia. See T.H. Robinson, *Prophecy and the Prophets in Ancient Israel* (London: Gerald Duckworth & Co. Ltd., 1967), 146f.

[186] Cited by H.H. Rowley, *Man of God: Study in Old Testament History and Prophecy* (London: Thomas Nelson & Sons Ltd., 1962), 169.

[187] Quoted by Ackroyd in *Exile and Restoration*, 103.

[188] This is advocated by McKenzie, Holladay, North, etc., See J.L. McKenzie, *Second Isaiah: Anchor Bible* (New York: Doubleday & Company Ltd., 1968), xviii., William L. Holladay, *Isaiah: Scroll of a Prophetic Heritage* (Grand Rapids, Michigan: Eerdmans, 1978), 16. Also See North, *The Second Isaiah*, 4.

[189] Duhm's thesis is challenged on various grounds: (a) each section of the prophecy is considered to have undergone successive redactions; (b) its unity with the other sections (1-39 and 55-66) is affirmed and (c) also the place of writing could possibly be Palestine. See discussion in Joseph Blenkinsopp, *A History of Prophecy in Israel,* 185ff.

it is generally agreed that Isaiah 40-55, called Second/Deutero-Isaiah comes from the exiles of Babylonia shortly before the dawn of Persian Empire.[190] The prophecy of Deutero-Isaiah is conceived of as a response to a kind of disillusionment about the faith of the Jewish people in the exile and refutations of the claims of Babylonian religion.[191] This prophecy therefore, will be taken as coming from an unknown prophet of the exilic age, whose work reflects the situations in the last part of the exile.

2.10. Responses to the Exiles in Exilic Prophets

The national disaster in the sixth century BCE was an unforgettable event for the Jewish community. It produced manifold reactions and responses to the exilic crisis within the members of the community. Priests, historians as well as prophets tended to answer a pertinent question: Why did such a tragic event occur to the people of God? What will be in the future? The voices of the prophets in this aspect are significant in various ways, which will be summarized as follows:

2.10.1. Exile as the Judgment of God

For the exilic prophets, the destruction of Jerusalem and the consequent exile is the judgment of God, which is a response to the faithlessness of the people of Judah. According to Jeremiah God is he who sent the agent of his judgment "from the north" that is Babylon (Jer. 4:5- 8; 5:15-17; 6:22-26). God is indeed the actor who brings disaster, but the people themselves are the cause (1:16; 7:5-10). For Jeremiah the day of the Lord would be a day of judgment (12:3).[192] His prophetic role in the royal court of Jehoiachim and Zedekiah involves counseling the royal court to be prepared for the coming doom (26:1; 27:6-7). The theme of the doom is also vividly

---

[190] Von Rad, *The Message of the Prophets*, 206.

[191] E.W. Heaton, *The Old Testament Prophets* (London: Darton, Longman & Todd, 1977), 107.

[192] According to Winfried Thiel, announcement of judgment is original to Jeremiah and a hope of restoration in Jeremiah is the Deuteronomist's insertion and the number seventy might have occurred to the Deuteronomistic redactor when Cyrus is appeared. Cited in Klein, *Israel In Exile*, 52.

portrayed in the symbolic actions.[193] Jeremiah focuses much of his attention to the leaders of Israel who bear the blame for defection (27:6). He encounters prophets of optimism who predict salvation to be imminent (6:14; 8:11; 23:27). His letter to a group of exiles in Babylonia to "build houses, plant gardens, get marry…" shows submission or non-violent resistance.[194] A call to submit to Babylon, to say yes to the reality and appropriation of God's judgment is Jeremiah's message as the shades of exile fell.

Like Jeremiah Ezekiel also announces Judah's doom as the righteous judgment of God. His prophecy against Judah is harsher in tone, and stronger in judgment than Jeremiah's, that the doom he felt compelled to announce evoked severe internal tensions, and, at times, left him physically incapacitated (24:27; 33:22). Much of his earlier prophecy is directed to proclaim that God's will was that Jerusalem should be besieged and destroyed (4-5). For him, the disaster was caused by the evils of its people's ways and was not to be regarded as an occasion for mourning, but as a proof of the working out of God's purposes (24:15-18). Ezekiel stands up to vindicate divine justice in the judgment of God (18:129). The reason for the punishment of Judah is expressed with different imageries.

2.10.2. Restoration of the Exiles

Exilic prophets are not only prophets of judgment, but also prophets and poet of hope. Jeremiah remembers that his call is not only to pluck up, to tear down…but also to plant and build (1:10). His message of judgment is also not entirely without hope, but utters "until" of new possibility (27: 7; 27:22). Von Rad is in the opinion that prophecies of salvation in Jeremiah is seen in his final period which is characterized by: (a) encouragement to those of exiles in Babylon (29:5-7), (b) promise of future hope (29:11), (c) a new

---

[193] These include the loincloth (13:1-11), the broken jar (19:1-3), and a pot of a potter (18:1-11).

[194] Scholars such as Duhm, Volz and Seidl believe the whole chapter except vv. 5-7 to be the editorial work that anticipated a hope of return. Thus attributing the original work (vv 5-7) to be original without hope of return. See Daniel L. Smith " Jeremiah as Prophet of Non-Violent Resistance," in *The Prophets (A Sheffield Reader)*, edited by Philip R. Davies (Sheffield: Sheffield Academic Press, 1999), 215.

Jerusalem (33:4ff; 31:6), (d) new covenant (31:31f.), (e) and a new ruler of Davidic house (30:9, 21).[195] A hope of restoration and re-establishment of the community is particularly elaborated in the oracular collection of 30-31.[196] Judgment of God to the exiles is to be fulfilled with "I will be your God and you will be my people" (7:23; 30:22). Thus, the tradition in the book of Jeremiah shows how various elements within the community's experience may be seen to link with hope - a hope which lies beyond the disaster and which is ultimately rooted in the enduring nature of divine promise, and expressed in terms of reversal of the words of doom on the basis of the bond with his people.

In the same manner Ezekiel's purpose was to assure the exilic community that the judgment of God is not finalized with judgment, but will be culminated with restoration (11:14-21). This is further elaborated in the second half of the book. This promise of restoration is proclaimed using significant themes that runs through the book as follows: (a) The rise of a more glorious temple which marks the dwelling or presence of God in the restored community (37:26f.).[197] (b) The promise of the land particularly its re-occupation frequently appears (34:25, 28). (c) Cult reform with new ways of cultic offering as the will of God is predicted (44:28-31 Cf.43: 7-8). (d) The promise of future Davidic king is portrayed with various imageries such as: a cedar planted on the top of mountain (17:22-24), the good shepherd (34:23f.), the prince (45:7). Israel will become a new community with the endowment of the Spirit of God (37: 1-28).

The prophetic call for Deutero-Isaiah is to pronounce freedom for the captives. The message of Deutero-Isaiah most immediately is, one of comfort to the beaten people. (42:1ff.) God would elevate another servant, Cyrus, upon whom the Spirit of God dwells to set the Israelites free (42:1; 43:13). Brueggemann ascribes Deutero Isaiah to be the supreme example of liberative poetic imagination in

---

[195] G. von Rad, *The Massage of the Prophets*, 161-188.

[196] The origin and unity of this oracular collection is much debated. However, it is the general view that in its present form it belongs after 587. See more details in Ackroyd, *Exile and Restoration*, 59.

[197] The more elaborate description of a new temple in the last chapters (40-43) signifies the saving act of God (28:24-26).

the Old Testament.[198] God had not abandoned Israel forever but he promised a glorious salvation for the remnant (exilic community) (54:7-8). God's act of salvation is not merely a reversal of divine policy, but rather creation of a new thing (43:19). Great stress was laid on Yahweh's reestablishment of his covenant with Israel which is giving a new obligation to Israel, that is, to declare and witness the universal plan of God to the nations (42:6; 49:6). Therefore, the ultimate response to the exiles in Deutero Isaiah is to comfort and make them rejoice in the divine judgment with the promise of a new messiah empowered with the Spirit of God. He deals with the doubts of the exiles that were challenged by the Babylonian gods and religion (41:1-5 Cf. Dan. 3).

2.10.3. Eschatological Hope in Exilic Prophets

As stated in the above, the main message of the exilic prophets is proclamation of divine judgment and promise of restoration. Their massages thus tend to have a forward look and thus eschatological hope is anticipated. Unlike the future concept of the pre-exilic prophets,[199] exilic prophets look forward beyond judgment upon Judah and of the foreign nations, but rather entail new covenant, new creation, and new exodus.[200] The future of Jeremiah entails a new covenant made by God with his people, different from the old Mosaic covenant in that Israel's will shall conform to Yahweh's will (Jer. 31:31ff.). The new age will be characterized by prosperity (Jer. 31:12). It belongs not to Israel alone nor to Judah but to both nations who together make up the ideal people of God (31:31).

For Ezekiel, the total people of God will be restored with the dynamic function of the Spirit of God (37:15-28). The dry bones that will be gathered together imply newness of life, a new body shaped by God (37:1-4). According to Lang, the hope of resurrection in Ezek. 37 involved not only restoration of Israel, but also the new

---

[198] Brueggemann, *Hopeful Imagination*, 96.

[199] For pre-exilic prophets the future always lay on the far side of judgment of God upon Israel and Judah when they believed that God would start all over again with Israel. (Cf. Hos. 2:15f; Isa. 9:9b-15; 11:1-9).

[200] See detailed discussion in Harry Mowvley, *Reading the Old Testament Prophets Today* (Atlanta: John Knox Press, 1979), 126-128.

Jewish commonwealth with some of the death.[201] Ezekiel teaches about the renewal of the centre of life by means of acquiring a new heart (11:19f; 36:26). Transformation of humanity will be realized with the gift of the divine spirit that arouses one to God's will (36:27). With Deutero-Isaiah we return to more far reaching views based upon past traditions. In the imminent return from Babylon to the homeland God will perform a new thing which will form the basis of the new community (43:18f.). The future appears to include the figure of the servant of Yahweh which may be thought of as a royal figure or as a prophetic, mosaic figure or, perhaps even more likely, as a new figure who combines within himself royal, prophetic and priestly traits (Cf. 42:1ff; 53:1-15). The new king would be endowed with the Spirit of God (42:1 cf. 61:1).

2.11. The Spirit of God in the Writings of Exilic Prophets

It is in the period of the exile that new developments of religious understanding had emerged including the understanding of the Spirit of God. Thus the term spirit is used in connection with God (thus Spirit of God) more than twenty times in the writings of exilic prophets.[202] As highlighted in the foregoing discussions, the Spirit of God in its earliest usage is a quasi-material energy producing results in human lives that have nothing essentially ethical or religious in their content.[203] By the time of prophets of the Exile, the idea of the Spirit (Spirit of God) is ethicized and spiritualized (Cf. Ezek. 36: 26).

While the great classical prophets of the pre-exilic period did not speak about the possession of the Spirit of God in order to

---

[201] Lang suggests that the hope of resurrection of the body was not originally a Jewish idea, but a doctrine borrowed from the ancient Iranians, first seen in the teaching of Zoroaster who lived sometime between 1400-600 BC. See Bernhard Lang, "Life after Death in the Prophetic Promise," *Supplement to Vetus Testamentum, Congress Volume: Jerusalem 1986*, edited by J.A. Emerton (Leiden: E.J. Brill, 1988), 154f.

[202] Direct reference to the *ruah* of God in Ezekiel is calculated to be seventeen. In Deutero Isaiah direct references are found five times. See references in Kohler and Baumgartner, "רוּחַ," *HALOT*, 1200f.

[203] E.F. Scott, *The Spirit in the New Testament*, 14ff.

justify or authenticate their vision,[204] prophetic literature of the exile frequently emphasizes prophecy as the obvious work of the Spirit of God (Ezek. 11:5; Isa. 48:16). Though the term Spirit of God is voided in Jeremiah, parallel references suggest distinctive uses of the spirit in relation to God.[205] The Spirit of God is used in connection with displacement of the prophet (Ezek. 3:12), with endowment of messianic king (Isa. 42:1). While the Spirit of God is mostly operating in relation to individual figures, exilic prophets declare that it will be poured upon the house/seed of Israel (Ezek. 49:29; Isa. 44:3). Being in the darkest hour of tragedy, prophets of the exilic period addressed the Spirit of God to be endowed upon the suffering people to restore and give new life (Ezek. 37:14 cf. Jer. 31:33).

The role of the Spirit of God in the writings of the exilic prophets involves ethical significance with establishment of justice upon all nations (Isa. 42:1). The references "his spirit" (Isa. 48:16) and "who has directed the Spirit Elohim" (Isa. 40:13) may have assumed the Spirit of God as an extension of Yahweh's personality. Subsequently, in the later period (post-exilic), the concept of Holy Spirit (Ps. 51:13; Isa. 63:10f) becomes a comprehensive theological concept, which simply refers to God. This may open up attributing all divine acts to the activity of the Holy Spirit in the New Testament.[206] Therefore, the understanding of Spirit of God in the writings of exilic prophets represents a clear shift with distinctive meaning and significance in the time of exile.

2.12. Summary

The foregoing study highlights the historical situation in the exilic period and also brings out certain elements of prophetic response to the exile. The study reveals that the life in the exile was neither

---

[204] Prophet's reserve about the Spirit may have been due to conflicts, which for some of them, Jeremiah in particular, had to suffer with the false prophets who boasted their possession of *ruah*. See Edmond Jacob, *Theology of the Old Testament*, 125.

[205] Cf. Jer. 4:11-12; 49:36; 51:1. This will be dealt with in the next chapter with detailed study of the use of *ruah* in Jeremiah.

[206] Pezhumkattil, "The Spirit as the Power of God in the Old Testament," *Bible Bhasyam* XIX/4 (December, 1993): 295.

extremely oppressive nor completely liberative. Exilic communities lost their socio-economic and political status and suffered a kind of rejection and oppression from powerful nations. The communities of both the exiles in Babylon and in the homeland were uprooted from their original social identity. The period on the other hand marks re-examination and reconstruction of their faith with creation of profound religious literatures.

Prophets of the period who shared the same fate warned, exhorted and comforted the suffering community and kindled hope of restoration in the minds of the exiles. They responded the catastrophe that it was God's judgment upon the people who sinned against him; but the sovereign God is going to deliver his people creating a new community. This promise of hope for the future is developed with characteristic features of eschatological tones. In the painful experiences of deportations and exiles, prophets of the same age brought out a distinctive religious teaching with a distinctive theological understanding of the Spirit of God. With the growing tradition of prophetic literature, the Spirit of God has become distinctive theological thought, with specific meaning and significance in the reshaping of Israel's religious tradition. This we will look upon in the following chapters.

Chapter 3

The Meaning and Significance of the Spirit of God in the Book of Ezekiel

3.1. Introduction

The book of Ezekiel is considered to be one of the writings of exilic prophets that contain varied theological ramifications responding to the theological crisis of the time. The book represents a number of references to the term "spirit" and the "Spirit of God." He stands as the exilic prophet of the Spirit par excellence.[207] The identification of the Spirit of God and the role played by the Spirit of God in the prophecy is very significant. Therefore, more space is devoted for the study in this chapter.

In the following study, attempt is made to delineate the meaning and significance of the Spirit of God in the book of Ezekiel. The following format is followed: 1) A brief introduction is given

[207] Quoted by Richard J. Sklba, "Until the Spirit from on High is Poured Out on Us (Isa. 32:15): Reflections of the Role of the Spirit in the Exile," *Catholic Bible Quarterly* 46/1 (January, 1984): 14.

in which the issues of authorship and composition, a brief survey of the ministry of the prophet and his locale of ministry, are dealt with.[208] 2) Exegesis of selected passages is the main part of the thesis. The format of the exegesis runs as: translation, text critical analysis, form critical analysis, and comments in relation to the meaning and significance of the Spirit of God. Since all the passages, which contain the Spirit of God, could not be dealt with in the exegetical study on account of limitation of space, the researcher limits the study to five passages to represent the book.

3.2. Authorship and Composition

The book of Ezekiel has been known to be one of the exilic literatures written by prophet Ezekiel who also experienced the exilic catastrophe. According to tradition, the book of Ezekiel has come down to us through Ezekiel, a prophet-priest who was exiled in 597 BCE along with king Jehoiakin and others. He received his call in Babylon in the year 593, and he exercised his office from then on until about 571 (Cf. 1:3; 29:17). Not until the close of the last century, serious criticism of the book had been anticipated.[209] However, the authenticity has been challenged since the early part of the last century. Scholars have been observing numerous repetitive doublets, and illogical breaks in the text and thereby suggest a late editorial compilation. Thus, the dominant idea among some of the scholars is that the book received its final and fullest redaction sometime in the postexilic period.[210] For Torrey, the prophecy is a

[208] The historical background of the prophecy is not dealt with in this introductory note as it is dealt with in chapter II of the thesis. See "The Historical Situations of the Exilic Age and the Prophetic Response."

[209] The general viewpoint at the end of the nineteenth century was summed up by S.R. Driver as: "No critical question arises in connection with the authorship of the book; the whole from the beginning to end bearing unmistakably the stamp of a single mind." See S.R. Driver, *Introduction to Literatures of the Old Testament* (New York: Meridian Books, 1956), 279.

[210] Holscher, Kessler, R. Kittel, C.C. Torrey, J. Smith, G.R. Berry, Irwin, Eichrodt, Brownlee, Greenberg and others agree that the authentic words of the prophet are the core of the prophecy and the final composition being in the hand of the later redactor which resulted in a remodeling, elaborating and supplementing of the original work. See William H. Brownlee, *Ezekiel 1-19: WBC Vol. 28* edited

late pseudepigraph on composed in the third century B.C, which consists of an imaginary prophecy by one of the unnamed prophet of Manasseh's reign.[211] While the authenticity is strongly challenged, scholars of the 1950s and 1960s dealt with the book's theological aspects. From this study it is observed that the prophecy addresses the exiles and hence it is authentic to the prophet.[212] The integration and close connection of the whole content is affirmed.[213] Therefore, the book is an outcome of a set of memoirs composed by the prophet himself and an inserted collection in the later days, which reflects the catastrophe of 587, more suitably the exiles in Babylonia.

3.3. The Ministry of the Prophet and Locale of His Ministry

One of the problems faced in the study of Ezekiel is the ambiguity of the life history of the prophet and his place of ministry. Scholars such as Torrey and others who deny the actual event of the exile question the prophetic ministry in the period of the exile.[214] Therefore, it is not easy to trace the life history of the prophet and the locale of his ministry. Statement in the book (1:1-3 & 29:17) places the prophet's period of activity between 574 and 571 BCE. He received his call

---

by David A. Hubbard et. al., (Waco, Texas: Word Books, Publisher, 1986), C.C. Torrey, *Pseudo-Ezekiel and the Original Prophecy* (New York: K. Tav Pub. House, Inc., 1970), W.A. Irwin, *The Problems of Ezekiel* (Chicago: Univ. of Chicago Press, 1943). Walter Eichrodt, *Ezekiel, A Commentary* (London: SCM Press Ltd., translated by Cosslet Quinn, 1970), Moshe Greenberg, *Ezekiel 1-20: Anchor Bible Vol. 20* (Garden City, New York: Doubleday & Co. Inc., 1983).

[211] See Torrey, *Pseudo-Ezekiel and the Original Prophecy*, 97ff. See also II Kings 21:10.

[212] The major studies which have appeared since 1950, those of Fohrer (1952), Zimmerli (1955), von Rabenau (1956), Graf von Reventlow (1962), and Howie (1950 & 1961) – are witnessing a return to something like the positions before 1930. See more detail in D.M.G. Stalker, *Ezekiel: Introduction and Commentary* (London: SCM Press Ltd., 1968), 18.

[213] See discussion in P.R. Ackroyd in *Exile and Restoration, A Study of Hebrew Thought of the Sixth Century* (London: SCM Press Ltd., 1968), 103.

[214] According to Torrey, the Biblical tradition about the exile and the restoration were an invention of the Chronicler to combat the claim of historical continuity made by the Samaritans. Cited by Moshe Greenberg in "Prolegomenon" *Pseudo-Ezekiel and the Original Prophecy*, xiii.

when he was a young man, probably at the age of thirty. So his youth fell in the period of the reformer king Josiah (639-609).[215] Like his contemporary Jeremiah, Ezekiel reacted against the tyrant rule of Jehoiakim at the eve of the first deportation. Ezekiel's prophecy in the early part of his ministry condemned breaking of an oath of allegiance with Babylonia.

At the time of Nebuchadnezzar's first deportation, the young Ezekiel was one of those who underwent the bitter fate of deportation. According to the biblical record, the prophet was deported in 597 to Babylon and prophesied in exile in the land of the Chaldeans by the river Chebar (1:3) at Tel-Abib (3:15). He received his call in Babylonia in the year 593 BCE (Cf. 1:1) and exercised his ministry till the year 571 (Cf. 29: 17).[216] It is traditionally assumed that Ezekiel, a priest-prophet exercised his ministry mainly in Babylonia. Some commentators assume that the prophet worked in Jerusalem until the fall of the city, then after a short stay in an unknown place in Palestine, he emigrated to Babylonia, where he subsequently received a second call and developed a second period of prophetic activity.[217] As we infer from our study of the situation of the exiles, we can assume that there would have been gatherings for worship and instructions in Babylonia, where prophet Ezekiel played important prophetic role. The prophet must have been responsible for fixing the forms of prayer, and instructions in to writing. The disciples who were gathered around him may be responsible to collect, copy out, and editing his writings so that a fixed tradition had emerged.

Many scholars have vigorously challenged the traditional picture that the prophet lived and prophesied in Babylonia during the exiles.[218] One of the major arguments for this stand is that

---

[215] See detailed discussion in Eichrodt, *Ezekiel, A Commentary,* 1ff.

[216] This calculation is based on the year of the reign of king Jehoiakin who became an exiled king of the Jewish community in Babylonia. This calculation is challenged by many scholars such as Burrows, Winckler, Smith, Berry, Torrey, etc. See John W. Wevers, *Ezekiel: The Century Bible* (London: Thomas Nelson & Sons, Ltd., 1969), 23f.

[217] Bertholet suggests this view. See Eichrodt, *Ezekiel, A Commentary*, 8.

[218] For example Heintrich, Bertholet, Mattthews, Torrey, Finkelstein, and Brownlee are among the scholars who rather favour Palestinian locale for the

chapters 1-24 is more relevant to Jerusalem and Judah rather than to exiles that the prophecy belongs to Jerusalem and Judah.[219] Reference to "the house of Israel" in many instances, the presence of the prophet in Palestine "in the midst of rebellious house" (12:2 cf. 3:17-21; 33:1-20), and intimate acquaintance with the moral, political and military conditions in Judah (Cf. 11: 15; 12:21-28) suggest a Palestinian locale. Brownlee argues that Ezekiel ministered from his home in Gilgal and that references to Gilgal were corrupted to *gola* "exile." From there Ezekiel delivered personally his prophecies against foreign nations. After prophesying in Egypt in 586 BCE, he led a group of exiles back to Gilgal. Thus, for Brownlee, Babylonian setting was introduced by a major revision in the late fourth century BC whose purpose was to defend the postexilic temple and the Jerusalemite priesthood.[220] While the view of Torrey and Brownlee wins certain support, most of the scholars hold the traditional view that Ezekiel ministered solely in Babylon before and after the exile.[221]

Wevers defends the possibility of Babylonian locale as follows: 1) The intimate knowledge of Jerusalem and Judah is possible as contact and correspondence between Jerusalem and Babylonia were possible during the time. 2) The exiles considered themselves part of the house of Israel, and hence the passages referring to "rebellious house" do not necessarily refers to Palestinian locale. 3) It is correct to maintain that a message directed to a society demands the physical presence of the prophet. Those who deny the Babylonian locale, in fact, do not represent clear and better stand to prove their thesis.

---

ministry of Ezekiel and the prophecy itself.

[219] Wevers, *Ezekiel*, 24. See also Moshe Greenberg, "Prolegomenon" *Pseudo-Ezekiel and the Original Prophecy*, xiii. Also Brownlee, *Ezekiel 1-19: WBC*, xxv.

[220] Brownlee suggests that the varied spellings of Gilgal, together with the geographic requirements of the book suggest that references to the גולה (exile) conceal the original mentions of Gilgal, Ezekiel's hometown. In the original consonantal spelling "to/at Gilgal" was written הגלגלה, whereas "the exile" was written הגלה. The former could easily be reduced to the latter, either through scribal error or through editorial activity. See Brownlee, *Ezekiel 1-19: WBC*, xxvf.

[221] This view is advocated by scholars such as Y. Kaufmann, G.C. Howie, Wevers, Cook, Eichrodt, Greenberg Boed, Vauter, and Hoppe. See Lotmar Eugene Cooper, Sr., *Ezekiel: NAC.* Vol. 17, edited by E. Ray Clendenen, et. al., (USA: Broadman & Holman Publishers, 1994), 34.

Therefore, we may conclude that the Babylonian locale of the ministry is more likely.

3.4. The Spirit of God in the Book of Ezekiel

The book of Ezekiel contains a number of references to the spirit and the Spirit of God. The term spirit occurs 52 times.[222] Out of these 52 occurrences, about 14 times is to be read as the Spirit of God.[223] Whatever the phrase may be, the book of Ezekiel contains quite a number of references to the Spirit of God and it has often been called the book of the Spirit of God par excellence. The term is translated in many ways including wind, breath, or spirit. The spirit plays a significant place in the oracles of Ezekiel where the lifeless and hopeless situations of the exiles were addressed. Therefore, it is relevant to have a look on the relevant passages in the book of Ezekiel in relation to the meaning and significance of the Spirit of God. This we will look through exegetical studies of relevant passages.

3.5. The Spirit of God - A Moving Force

3.5.1. Text: Ezekiel 3:12-15

v. 12: Then the spirit lifted me up, and (I heard) behind me a voice of a great rushing, saying[a] "the glory of the Lord rose from its place"[a]

v. 13: Then I heard the sound of the wings of the living creatures touching one another, and a sound of[a] the wheels side by side, and a sound of[b] a great[c] earthquake.

v. 14: Then the spirit lifted me up and took me away and I went in bitterness[a] in the [b]heat of my spirit,[b] but the hand of the Lord was strong upon me.

---

[222] Ludwig Kohler and Walter Baumgartner, "רוח," *Hebrew and Aramaic Lexicon of the Old Testament* Vol. 2., translated and edited by M.E.J. Richardson, (Leiden: Brill, 2000), 1197.

[223] The number of occurrences could not be exactly ascertained because exegetes are not in the same opinion in attributing certain references whether to read as the *ruah* of God or not. For example Baumgartel lists 11 occurrences of the *ruah* of God in the book of Ezekiel, Kohler and Baumgartner list 17. See Baumgartel, "Spirit in the Old Testament" *TDNT* Vol. 6, edited by Gerhard Friedrich, translated by Geoffrey E. Bromiley (Grand Rapids, Michigan: Eerdmans, 1968), 360. Also Kohler and Baumgartner, "רוח," *HALOT*, 1200f.

v. 15: Then I came to the exiles at Tel-abib, [a]who dwells by the river Chebar[a] [b]and I sat where they sat, and remain there[b] being devastated[d] in their midst for seven days.

3.5.2. Text Critical Notes

v. 12 [a-a] Literally "blessed be the glory ..." Luzzato and Hitzig independently propose conjectural emendation ברום as "arose" from רום instead of the MT ברוך "blessed be." The verse will therefore be "when the majesty of the Lord rose from its place.[224] Brownlee further comments that the error is graphically feasible, that is a confusion of ב and מ in the archaic script, which concurs with its antedating the ancient versions. If we compare with other visionary experience of the prophets (e.g., Isaiah chapter 6) the same use of רום "to exalt/lift up" could be acknowledged. Thus, the emendation is more likely.

v. 13 [a-b] In this verse we have וְ in three instances. They are explicative.[225] The BHS suggests to delete ו in this clause to read as "...and a sound of the wheels touching side by side sounded like a great quake."

v.13 [c] the adjective "great" is lacking in the original Greek text (LXX). The MT reading needs no emendation as it expresses the intensity of the earthquake. While Eichrodt, de Wette and Zimmerli delete it as secondary, Brownlee defends the authenticity, drawing attention to the chiastic arrangement of vv 12-14.[226]

v.14 [a] מר (bitterness) is lacking in certain versions and manuscripts including the Greek original and Syriac. Zimmerli regards it as an incorrect explanation of the following phrase in terms of bitter anger instead of exultation.[227] Wevers suggests to retain it in view of the possibility of word play on bitterness and rebellious, i.e., מר and מרי.[228] Block prefers to take the root from the Ugaritic word

---

[224] This is also adopted in RSV and NEB. See Brownlee, *Ezekiel 1-19: WBC*, 36.

[225] See Brown Driver Briggs, *Lexicon*, 252. Also see Greenberg, *Ezekiel 1-20*, 71.

[226] Brownlee, Ezekiel *1-19 WBC*, 36. Cf. Daniel I. Block, *The Book of Ezekiel 1-24: NICOT*, edited by R.K. Harrison (Grand Rapids, Michigan: Eerdmans, 1997), 132.

[227] Cited by Brownlee, *Ezekiel 1-19: WBC*, 37.

[228] Wevers, *Ezekiel*, 55.

mrr "to be strengthened/empowered" thus producing for the clause, "I went forth strengthened in the fervour of my spirit."[229] The MT is still appropriate.

v.14 [b-b] The term חמה (heat) occurs 32 times in the book and points to divine anger except in this verse. The LXX translates it with orgh (impulse/passion). The phrase means, "it is the glow of his spirit , which arose as a consequence of seizure by the spirit/hand of God."

v. 15 [a-a] RSV omits the phrase "who dwells by the river Chebar." The omission may be correct as it seems to be an expansion of the later writer on the basis of 1:3.

v. 15 [b-b] Literally this line runs as "and I sat where they sat; and I sat (remained) there where they sat (there)." There are four clauses that appear to be a conflation of two readings joined by w. Cook argues that one or the other of these sentences must be a gloss, though Greek recognizes both.[230] The qere tries to make sense of the conflation by adopting ואשר "and who/where" to ואשב "and I sat" Most scholars adopt only one clause, either the first (Fohrer, RSV, NEB) or the second (Zimmerli, Greenberg, BHS).[231]

v. 15 [d] Instead of משים (hiph. ptc – having devastated) the proposed reading is משומם (Poal ptc. – being devastated/appalled). The same use being represented in Ezra 9:3f. Greenberg finds parallel in Jer. 15:17 where the verse represents physical and emotional meanings.[232] The emendation is recommendable.

3.5.3. Form Critical Notes

Ezekiel 3:12-15 has been treated as the conclusion or completion of the commissioning of the prophet. It is a scholarly consensus that a bulk of passages, 1:1-3:15 forms Ezekiel's inaugural vision and

[229] Cited by Cooper, *Ezekiel: NAC*, 83.

[230] G.A. Cook, *The Book of Ezekiel: ICC* (Edinburgh: T&T Clark, 1936), 43.

[231] See Brownlee, *Ezekiel 1-19: WBC*, 37. Brownlee suggests that the latter is more likely.

[232] See Greenberg, *Ezekiel 1-20*, 72.

commission.[233] The pericope of the unit (vv.12-15) is characterized by the change of emphasis from the formal commissioning of the prophet to emphasize on the active involvement of the spirit which moved the prophet. Greenberg puts 3:12-15 as an end of the call scene. According to him, the skeleton of the narrative is carried by the verbs "I lifted ... I took ... I went... I came... I sat...," which is filled out by what may be a gloss in vv. 12b and 13.[234] In spite of possible gloss in this passage, the inaugural vision and commission has integrity in form and content.[235]

One can argue that not only the initial vision of the prophet in chapter 1 but also the commission itself (3:12-15) was part of the ecstatic experience where the Spirit of God moved the prophet from one place to another. Thus, the unit represents the original core in which the prophetic vision report is the genre of the passage. The unit can be structured as follows: The displacement of the prophet and experience of the great rushing (v.12), the prophet's exclamation of what he hears (v.13), the spirit picking up the prophet and carrying him off to Tell-abib (14-15).

With regard to the setting of the pericope, there have been two opposing streams: Those who deny the prophet's activity in Babylonia argue the prophecy to be a Jerusalemite origin or possibly a Babylonian redaction in a late period.[236] On the other hand as pointed out in the introduction, the Babylonian locale and the possible prophetic ministry in Tel-Abib in the river Chebar is agreeable. The setting of the prophetic call and commissioning could

---

[233] See Katheryn Pfisterer Darr, "The Book of Ezekiel" *The New Interpreter's Bible* Vol. VI, edited by Leander E. Keck et. al., (Nashville: Abingdon Press, 2001), 1607.

[234] According to Greenberg, vv. 12b and 13 are explicative statements which repeat the elements of the vision of chapter 1. The repetition thus elaborates the initial call of Chapter 1. See Greenberg, *Ezekiel 1-20*, 74. Other commentators such as Zimmerli and Wevers assign the verses (esp v. 13) as a gloss. See Wevers, *Ezekiel*, 54-55.

[235] The stylistic features and careful structure of the call and commissioning scene of 1:1-3:15 indicate its general integrity. See detailed discussion in Greenberg, *Ezekiel 1-20*, 74f.

[236] See Brownlee, *Ezekiel 1-19: WBC*, xxvif.

be Babylonia. The exact date and location is not known. The date according to 1:2 is 593/2 BCE, and hence it may be the early part of the exile, before the final fall of Jerusalem.[237]

3.5.4. Comments in Relation to the Meaning and Significance of the Spirit of God

The principal element of the section is the description of the prophet's conveyance to his place of ministry. This is found in vv. 12a, and 14-15a. The scene opens with Ezekiel being lifted up off his feet by a " spirit " which Brownlee translates as "spirit-wind."[238] The prophet was lifted up by the spirit, the same activating force of chapter 2: 2. In contrast to the internal energizing activity of the spirit in 2:2, here the prophet is acted upon from the outside, apparently like a scrap of paper picked up by a gust of wind.[239] While the exact phrase Spirit of God is not mentioned, the transportation of the prophet back from Jerusalem to Chaldea (Babylonia) is described as wrought by the "Spirit Elohim" in 11:24. The same visionary experience appeared in 37:1 where the hand of God was upon the prophet and the Spirit Elohim brought him out in the middle of the valley of dry bones. In any case the activity of the Spirit of God upon Ezekiel is certain. Ezekiel senses himself being picked up by the Spirit of God even though he describes himself as going (v.14) and coming (v.15) and sitting (v.15) in his visionary experience.

The effect of the moving force is also attested by elements like hearing the sound of a great quake, beholding the glory of Yahweh

---

[237] The text provides the date "in the thirtieth year" (1:1) and "fifth year" (1:2). This is problematic and scholars differ in their interpretations. Some argues for the "thirtieth year" to be the age of the prophet (Budde), some other for the date of Josianic reform (Cooper, Brownlee), others as the date of publication of the completed book (Albright, Howie). The explanation (vv.2-3) takes the thirtieth year as another era equivalent to the fifth year of Jehoiachin's exile. Therefore, the possible date may be the thirtieth year (after the reform of Josiah – 621), in the fifth year (of the reign of Jehoiachin – who came to power in 597), in the fourth month (July).

[238] Brownlee, *Ezekiel 1-19: WBC*, 25.

[239] Cf. the function of *ruah* as a violent and powerful agent of displacement in Exodus 10:13, 19, Isa. 57:13; Dan. 2:35.

(v.12), proclamation of exclamation (v.13), and embittered in the fury of his spirit (v. 13). The transportation of the prophet back to Tel-abib raises a problem since the call and vision came while he was in a canal. Block's comment is likely that "by the river Chebar" in 1:1-3 is interpreted as a general designation for the area where the exile resided, and the river canal is an isolated place where the prophet received the vision.[240] There have been diverse interpretations for the meaning of "lifting up by the spirit." Some have argued that it is an ecstatic experience of feeling oneself as under the control of Yahweh.[241] It is simply a prophetic exaltation of the effect of ecstatic experience.[242] Most of the scholars, however, accept the role of the Spirit of God in displacing the prophet. Thus, the Spirit of God, the same activating force of 2:2, 8:3; 37:1 took Ezekiel out of his compatriots to be used by Yahweh. The arrival and departure of the divine vehicle (spirit) mark off the event of the prophet's call. Greenberg comments that the theophany gains other particular signification in the time of exile.

Ezekiel as a prophet ought to prove himself divinely inspired, and this was done by this visionary experience.[243] Thus the Spirit of God is a moving force responsible for the strong impulse given to the prophet so that he may accomplish the divine commission. The Spirit of God distanced and separated the prophet from his people inwardly and physically. While staying among his people, he was separated to operate in another realm, a zone governed by divine realities, so that he became a man totally possessed by the Spirit of God.

---

[240] Block, *Ezekiel 1-24*, 136.

[241] Cooke, *The Book of Ezekiel: ICC*, 42. Cooke interprets that this phrase implies that the vision departs, and the prophet sets out, still under the influence of his ecstasy.

[242] Joseph Blenkinsopp, *Ezekiel: Interpretation: A Bible Commentary for Teaching and Preaching* (Louisville: John Knox Press, 1990), 27f. Blenkinsopp denies that the vision has been appended to the commissioning.

[243] Greenberg, *Ezekiel 1-20*, 79ff.

3.6. The Spirit of God - An Inspiring Force

3.6.1. Text: Ezekiel 11:4-6

v. 4: Therefore [a]prophesy unto them prophesy[a] O mortal one

v. 5: Then the spirit[a] of the Lord fell upon me[a] and said to me[b], "[c]Speak, thus says the Lord[c]; this is what you think, O house of Israel; I know[d] what is [e]the thought of your spirit[e].

v. 6: [a]You have multiplied your slain in this city and filled up its streets with the slain.

3.6.2. Text Critical Notes

v. 4 [a-a]The verb form הנבא עליהם הנאב (prophesy unto them prophesy) is used twice in relation to the prophet for emphasis and to stress the urgency of the assignment.[244]

v. 5 [a-a] xwr is lacking in the original Greek. While Zimmerli treats the statement as a later addition because of breaking up divine speech in this verse,[245] the statement is unique in the book and is authentic. The verb נפל is used elsewhere concerning the hand of Yahweh. It appears a redundant, since the prophet is already engaged in a spirit filled experience.

v. 5 [b] *and said to me* is absent in Greek original text, but is needed on account of chiasm.

v. 5 [c-c] This phrase is to be emended as "prophesy and speak" (Zimmerli). According to Brownlee, the command has been misplaced from its original position at the beginning of the chapter.[246] The emendation by Zimmerli is a likely reading.

v. 5 [d] According to Block, the suffix attach to ידע in this verse is a dittography influenced by the following letter "what is in your ...," therefore, the better rending is ידעתי "I know."[247]

v. 5 [e-e] ומעלות רוחכם אני רוחכם The rendering "but I know the thoughts of your spirit " is parenthetical or explanatory.[248] Brownlee

---

[244] Cooper, *Ezekiel: NAC*, 140.

[245] Cited by Block, *Ezekiel 1-24*, 327.

[246] Brownlee, *Ezekiel 1-19: WBC*, 158.

[247] Block, *Ezekiel 1-24*, 328.

[248] Cf. Cooper, *Ezekiel: NAC*, 141.

translates, "Thus you think, O Israel for the thoughts of your mind I know." The adjectival suffix ומעלות is emended by the BHS as ומעלת (Hiph. Part. Sing. fem. const. of מעלה which means being caused to exalt or lifted. Thus, it means the lofty mind or spirit .

v. 6 [a]The hiphil form "you have multiplied" is a causative of חרב and literally be translated: "you cause to be great/many." Thus it could be rendered as increase, multiply or make great.

3.6.3. Form Critical Notes

The book of Ezekiel chapter 11 is often known as vision of judgment and hope. In this chapter, scholars maintain two major divisions with other minor sub-divisions. Again each section is sub-divided depending on the form of the speech and contents. Scholars are not in the same opinion to the nature and design of the prophecy. Blenkinsopp, Cooper and Greenberg find the prophecy within the context of Temple vision (8:1-11:25).[249] On the other hand scholars such as Block, Wevers, Coote, Howie and Stalker set off the prophecy found in chapter 11 from the Temple vision.[250] The section 11:1-12 and the unit vv 4-6 is acknowledged quite distinctively from the temple vision (8-10) because of difference in structure, literary styles and contents as well as unity of 11:1-12 in a dramatic character of the vision.[251] Though the prophetic experience in this unit of the prophecy is closely associated with the larger temple vision, the unit may be treated as a separate ecstatic vision inserted into the account of temple vision.

The smaller unit of vv 4-6 is characterized by לכן (therefore), (v. 4) with the imperatives which functions as introductory note. The end of the unit is also to be noted when לכן (in v. 7) introduces a new topic, divine retribution to the house of Israel. The unit reflects the command of Ezekiel to prophesy against the people who utter,

---

[249] See Blenkinsopp, *Ezekiel,* 52, Greenberg, *Ezekiel 1-20,* 192, Cooper, *Ezekiel: NAC,* 138.

[250] See Block, *Ezekiel 1-24,* 328, C.G. Howie, *Ezekiel, Daniel: Layman's Bible Commentary* (London: SCM Press Ltd., 1961), 32, Stalker, *Ezekiel,* 108, and Wevers, *Ezekiel,* 92.

[251] For example, while Chaps. 9-10 assumes Jerusalem being destroyed; this chapter assumes that it still stands. See more detail in Block, *Ezekiel 1-24,* 329.

"the time is not near to build houses..." (v. 3), who are now called the house of Israel. The unit runs as follows: The command to prophesy (v.4) followed by the assertion of falling of the Spirit of God upon the prophet (v. 5a). This is followed by words of charge against the house of Israel (v. 5b). Verse 6 adds the words of condemnation.[252]

With regard to the genre, the unit represents a typical prophetic disputation speech, involving the explicit quotation of a popular opinion that demands explicit exposure and refutation.[253] In the preceding verses the opinion is set as "... they say that..." and the opinion continues here in v.5b "this is what you think."

As form critical analysis separates the unit from the temple vision, the occasion of the prophecy might be after an event of the temple vision which is expected to have taken place in the year 592 BCE.[254] The thought of the verses (11:1-12) suggests that Jerusalem was still standing, and the prophet had little hope of any remnant remaining outside the Chebar (v. 13). Thus the passage reflects situations prior to the final destruction of Jerusalem. Cooke and others believe that the prophecy received later redaction.[255] Seeing the disputation speech in the passage, one could have concluded that the context of 11:1-12, and particularly 4-6, which calls forth the prospect and denunciation of the leaders was between 597 and 587, possibly immediately after the event of 597. The place of the vision is difficult to tell with precision, it is possibly in Babylonia.

---

[252] Brownlee follows this structural pattern. See *Ezekiel 1-19: WBC*, 157f.

[253] The prophetic disputation speech is frequently related to the trial genres in that they are designed to argue against a particular viewpoint and thereby support the interrogations that take place in a courtroom setting. For Graffy, the structure of this form comprises two elements (a) the quotations of the opinion to be disputed and, (b) the refutation of the opinion. See Marvin A. Sweeney, *Isaiah 1-39 with an Introduction to Prophetic Literature* (Grand Rapids, Michigan: Eerdmans, 1996), 28.

[254] As suggested by Ezekiel 8:1 the vision was experienced in the sixth year, sixth month on the fifth day. Taken to read the year basing on the year of Jehoiakin's exile, the vision took place in September 18, 592 BCE. See discussion in Block, *Ezekiel 1-24*, 278.

[255] According to Cooke, the vision may have been seen just before the catastrophe of 586 BCE; and written down rather later. See *The Book of Ezekiel: ICC*, 121. Wevers also assigns vv. 9-10 to reflect the events of 586. See *Ezekiel*, 92.

3.6.4. Comments in Relation to the Meaning and Significance of the Spirit of God

The command to prophesy and refutation of Israel's sin seen in this passage is significantly portrayed as the prophet's experience of special inspiration and prophetic empowerment of the Spirit of God. The command for proclamation is given with emphasis, "prophesy, prophecy" which according to Block reflects the intensity of the provocation and the divine sense of insurgency.[256] Simultaneously with the divine command, the prophet experiences special inspiration and prophetic empowerment as the Spirit of God falls upon him.[257]

In vv. 1-3 we see the wicked leaders of Judah who gave wicked counsel in the city. The prophet has now addresses the counsel in v. 4 whose inner thought of mind (spirit) is known. Here in v. 4 the point of inspiration of the Spirit of God is manifested as the prophet is going to prophesy.[258] This reveals that until the Spirit of God inspires the prophet, no word is uttered. There is a play on word on spirit in this passage. While spirit functions as the agency of conveyance in v. 1, and in 5a as the agency of inspiration and in 5b it denotes the seat or organ of mental activity.[259] According to Block the description of the activity of the Spirit of God in 5a is significant as "to fall upon" stands midway between the energetic "to leap upon" (I Sam 10:6) and the more subdued form "to come upon" (I Sam 18:10).[260] For Cooke the statement "the Spirit of God falls upon me" implies that while he was still in his trance he receives an inspiration to prophesy.[261] But Wevers denies this statement in the sense of prophetic inspiration as

256 Block, *Ezekiel 1-24*, 334.

257 In our foregoing survey we have found that the reforming prophets hesitate to authenticate their prophecy as wrought by the *ruah* of God. See discussion in "Prophecy in the Pre-exilic classical prophets."

258 Brownlee suggests that until this point the prophet has not addressed the council, and this shows that until the *ruah* of God is upon the prophet, inspiration is not achieved. See Brownlee, *Ezekiel 1-19: WBC*, 158.

259 In v. 5b *ruah* serves as a variant for לֵב heart and it indicates that Yahweh is aware of the motives of the leaders of Judah. Cf. Block, *Ezekiel 1-24*, 335.

260 Block, *Ezekiel 1-24*, 334.

261 Cooke, *The Book of Ezekiel: ICC*, 122.

it is hardly in keeping with the divine activity for the divine spirit.[262] Brownlee acknowledges that a new context was ingeniously formed for the Spirit of God, as an introduction to an inspired speech of the prophet.[263]

We see here a theological development in the thinking of the prophet in the relationship between the "hand of God and the "Spirit of God," which are used synonymously. Keil argues that instead of the "hand" of God (8:1) the Spirit of Jehovah is mentioned here, because what follows is simply a divine inspiration.[264] Thus, the activity of the Spirit of God confirmed that the prophetic power is not attained in a magical or psychological sense, but inspired by God. Therefore, the Spirit of God that falls upon the prophet is an inspiring force for prophecy.

3.7. The Spirit of God – A Transforming Power

3.7.1. Text Ezekiel 36:24-28

v. 24: For I will take you from the nations, and gather you from all[a] the *countries and I will bring you into your own land.*

v. 25: Then I will sprinkle[a] clean water upon you and you shall be clean from all your uncleanness, and[b] I will cleanse you[b] from all your idols.

v. 26: I will give you [a]a new heart and a new spirit[b] I will put within you and I shall take away the [c]heart of stone from you and I will give you a heart of flesh[c].

v. 27: I will put my spirit within you and [a]I shall make you follow[a] my statue and be careful to keep my ordinances.

v. 28: Then you shall dwell in the land, which I [a] gave to your fathers, and you shall be my people and I will be your God.

---

[262] Wevers, *Ezekiel*, 93.

[263] Brownlee, *Ezekiel 1-19: WBC*, 157.

[264] Karl Friedrich Keil, *Biblical Commentary of the Prophecies of Ezekiel* Vol. I, translated by James Martin (Edinburgh: T&T Clark, MDCCCLXXVI), 146.

3.7.2. Text Critical Notes

v. 24 [a] In the plural noun הארצות some readings of the Cairo Geniza and Syriac add "מן" (from) suppressing כל in the preceding word.

v. 25 [a] Targum interprets וזרקתי (I will sprinkle) in connection with Numb. 19 "and will forgive your sins, even as they are cleansed with the water of sprinkling and with the ashes of the cow of the sin-offering." The verb is a figurative expression for cleansing,[265] but is rather a comment on the text. The interpretation needs not be retained.

v. 25 [b-b] Literally "I will make you clean" Syriac abbreviates it by omitting יטהרתם. In its place Syriac puts אידכי יתכון at the beginning of 25b. LXX adds a copula making the final verb independent, "You shall be clean from all your uncleanness and from all your idols; I will cleanse you." However, the MT needs no emendation.

v. 26 [a] Allen translates it as plural "hearts" arguing that a singular is used only where a part of the body is common to a number of persons.[266] But the emendation is not agreeable on the grounds of chiastic arrangement (heart and spirit).

v. 26 [a-b] new heart and new spirit (רוח and לב) are taken as parallel and synonyms.[267] The two terms though seen as virtual synonyms, the synonymity is not exact in the parallelism and here, the new heart is "given to" (נתן ל) and the spirit is put within (בקרב ב) them. A distinction is confirmed by the manner in which vv. 26b-27 elaborate on the two statements.

v. 26 [c-c] heart of stone...heart of flesh literally reads, "... from a stone from your heart I will give to you a heart of flesh." Targum reads "a godless heart which is hard as stone" and "a heart, fearful of me to do my will." But this is a comment on the

---

[265] Cooke, *The Book of Ezekiel: ICC*, 391.

[266] Leslie C. Allen, *Ezekiel 20-48: WBC*, edited by David A. Hubbard, et. al., (Dallas, Texas: Waco Books, Publisher, 1990), 176.

[267] The two terms taken together represent the person's internal locus of emotion, will and thought. Thus לב and רוּחַ are practically synonymous with each other. Cited by C.H. Toy, *The Book of the Prophet Ezekiel: A New English Translation with Explanatory Notes* (London: James Clarke & Co., 1899), 171.

text. A plain reading would be "and I will remove the heart of stone... and give you a heart of flesh."

v. 27 [a-a] אשר־בחקי תלכו is literally to be translated "which in my statue you shall go." The sentence structure follows a pattern of 'object-clause introduced by אֲשֶׁר'[268] The clause אֲשֶׁר is preceded by אֵת thus equivalent to "to walk" or more plainly "to follow."

v. 28 [a] Few readings of Cairo Geniza manuscripts have ואני instead of ואנכי. Only here in the book of Ezekiel does the long form occur.[269] The use of ואנכי in this verse is a conscious archaism in the covenant formula than evidence of a non-Ezekielian hand or Jeremianic influence.[270] Thus it is a formulaic expression of covenant in the prophecy.

3.7.3. Form Critical Notes

Scholars are not in the same opinion regarding the structural division of Ezekiel chapter 36. Majority of the exegetes put Ezekiel 36: 1-38 into two major sections (vv. 1-15 & vv. 16-38) which are composed into other minor sub-divisions. There is a general consensus on the unity of the section (vv. 16-38), which has been generally known as "Restoration of Israel."[271] Eichrodt is the one who separates the unit vv. 24-28 as "actual new creation of Israel" from a larger section.[272] Stalker and Block also separate the unit and call it "Transformation of

---

[268] On the construction see A.E. Cowley, *Gesenius' Hebrew Grammar*, Edited and Enlarged by E. Kautsch (Oxford: Clarendon Press 1910), 491.

[269] Cited by Walter Zimmerli, *Ezekiel 2: A commentary on the Book of the Prophet Ezekiel Chapters 25-48*, translated by James D. Martin, edited by Paul D. Hanson with Leo Jay Greenspoon (Philadelphia: Fortress Press, 1983), 243. *Ezekiel 2*, 243.

[270] See detailed discussion in Block, *Ezekiel 1-24*, 357.

[271] Scholars are slightly differing in their entitlement of the section. For example, Zimmerli describes it, "Israel's New life and the Free Gift of the God Who is True to Himself." Block calls, "The Transformation of Israel." Cooper calls, "Future Restoration of Fruitfulness in Israel." Stalker, "The Transformation of the People." Wevers calls it, "The Divine Basis for Restoration."

[272] Eichrodt, *Ezekiel*, 497.

Israel."[273] Therefore, Ezekiel 36:24-28 represents a clear demarcated textual unit, which however is part of a larger section of vv. 16-36, which concerns the promised restoration. Allen recognizes that the unit 24-28 indicates how Israel's history in the land may be prevented from repeating itself.[274] The unit may be structured as: The exiles will return to the land (v. 24), they will be cleansed (v. 25), the outpouring of the Spirit of God is announced (vv. 26-27), and the covenant will be renewed (v. 28).

With regard to the genre, 36:16-38 has been characterized as a disputative stylized salvation oracle.[275] Though the central issue is not the deliverance of Israel, the vindication of the reputation of Yahweh is reflected in the passage. The oracles in vv. 16-38 presuppose the exiles in specific spiritual distress. It is a serious question about the efficacy on the part of their God if they are Yahweh's people whom God led them out of Egypt. The oracle thus answers the problem of exiles, which represents a real spiritual distress. Therefore, fixing the period for the oracle cannot go beyond the time of the first return or perhaps of the rebuilding of the temple.[276] The oracle is possible to be dated further into the period of the exile rather than the early period immediately after the destruction of Jerusalem as it shares similar themes with that of Deutero-Isaiah and Jeremiah 31:31-34.[277]

Hermann suggests a redactional work for the oracle, particularly the deliverance oracle of vv. 26-27 in the late exilic period.[278] The issue of setting is further complicated by the omission of vv. 23b-38 in the oldest Greek text, suggesting that the unit may be a later

---

[273] See Stalker, *Ezekiel*, 252. Daniel I. Block, *The Book of Ezekiel 25-48: NICOT*, edited by R.K. Harrison (Grand Rapids, Michigan: Eerdmans, 1998), 354. According to Block, 25-28 forms a unit.

[274] Allen, *Ezekiel 20-48: WBC*, 179.

[275] Block, *The Book of Ezekiel 25-48*, 343. Block argues the theme of the passage in terms of Yahweh's honour in - crisis, recovery, and vindicated.

[276] Zimmerli, *Ezekiel 2*, 245.

[277] The concerns of those preachings are: a question of rebuilding of Jerusalem, a question of repopulation, promise of fruitfulness, hope for the returning exiles etc. See more detail in Zimmerli, *Ezekiel 2*, 246.

[278] Cited by Paul Joyce, *Divine Initiative and Human Response in Ezekiel* (Sheffield: Sheffield Academic Press, 1989), 116.

addition.[279] In view of these doubts, the late exilic date is most likely and it suggests the school of Ezekiel rather than Ezekiel himself as the author. However, Zimmerli's comment is recommendable when he says, "All the oracles will have to be derived from the prophet's exilic environment."[280]

3.7.4. Comments in Relation to the Meaning and Significance of the Spirit of God

Transformation of the exiles will be achieved with Yahweh's restorative actions of the exiles. This will begin with the gathering of his people from all the countries into their own land (v. 24). But Yahweh's efforts to vindicate his reputation will go far beyond merely re-unity, people and land; he will also revitalize the relationship between himself and his people.

Thus the promise in this oracle envisions a wholesale transformation of the nation,[281] or focuses on eschatological dimension.[282] Yahweh's restorative action will thus first gather the exiles (v. 24) and then purify Israel to its defilement with clean water so that they will be clean (טהר) (v. 25).[283] Secondly, Yahweh will remove a stony heart and replace it with a new heart (לב) and a new spirit (v. 26). According to Wevers, a heart of stone represents the inward impulse to disobedience which characterized Israel before and during exile.[284] The change of stony heart in Jeremiah 31:31-34 is associated with the covenant, but here with new heart and new

---

[279] See the argument with regard to eschatological nature of the passage in Johan Lust, "Ezekiel 34-40 in the Oldest Greek Manuscript" *Catholic Bible Quarterly* 43/4 (October, 1981): 517-533.

[280] Zimmerli, *Ezekiel 2*, 246.

[281] So Block argues it. See *The Book of Ezekiel 25-48*, 354.

[282] This is argued by Cooper. See, *Ezekiel: NAC*, 316.

[283] While the reference was to ceremonial cleansing that as necessary to reestablish worship (Num. 19:13, 20), it is important to note that the reference here is of internal rite. This signifies transformation of inner life of the individual more than restoration of the exiles. See Cooper, *Ezekiel: NAC*, 316.

[284] Wevers, *Ezekiel*, 274.

spirit.[285] Thus, there is a significant emphasis on the change of Israel in this verse (v. 26) and in the preceding verse. In verse 27 we see the transforming role of the Spirit of God more explicitly where we see the expression "the Spirit of God will move them to follow his laws." Allen makes a comment that the lives of Israel would be governed by a new impulse that was to be the expression of Yahweh's own Spirit. He would remake their human natures so that they marched to the music of the covenant terms that expressed Yahweh's nature and will.[286]

Verse 28 states that only due to the transforming power of the Spirit of God could the covenant relationship become a living actuality, and only thus could the old ideal of Yahweh's people in Yahweh's land become a reality. Block argues that this passage entails that regeneration was achieved not by works of righteousness but by Yahweh's infusion of the individual with his Spirit. Yahweh's putting a new spirit within them suggests that Yahweh himself is made to participate more directly within the people's new response.[287] Howie comments that in these verses Ezekiel deals with the most popular and pressing theological problem, which arose out of the destruction of Jerusalem and the experience of exile.[288] It was plain to see that Judah's sin; her abrogation of the covenant, was the basis for judgment, and rightly so. God's purpose in the restoration of his chosen nation was the revelation of himself to all people. Ezekiel, like Jeremiah, understood that a real change in the life of a person had to begin at the motive centre of personality; so he predicts the ideal future of a basic change in human nature, The change of personality (new heart, new spirit) which will result in restoration, and it is to be

---

[285] The difference of "giving new heart" and "putting new *ruah*" is well defined that new heart is given to, and new *ruah* is put within. The provision of new heart involves a removal of the petrified organ and its replacement with a heart of flesh, the source of which is unspecified. But the new *ruah* placed inside Israel is identified as Yahweh's *ruah*, which animates and vivifies the recipients. See Block, *The Book of Ezekiel 25-48*, 356.

[286] Allen, *Ezekiel 20-48: WBC*, 179.

[287] M.E. Andrew, *Responsibility and Restoration: The Course of the Book of Ezekiel* (Dunedin, New Zealand: University of Otago Press, 1985), 187.

[288] Howie, *Ezekiel, Daniel*, 72.

done by the Lord who will infuse his spirit in human beings. Ezekiel anticipates the transformation of inner lives of his compatriots so that restoration of the exilic community will be achieved with the transforming power of the Spirit of God.

3.8. The Spirit of God – A Life-giving Power

3.8.1. Text: Ezekiel 37:11-14

v. 11: *Then he[a] said to me, "Mortal, these bones are the houses of Israel. Behold[b] they say, "our bones are dried up, and[c] our hope is perished and [d]we are cut down[d]."*

v. 12: *Therefore prophesy and say to them[a], Thus says the Lord God,[b] Behold, I am opening your graves and I will bring you up from your graves, O my people[c] I wil bring you to the land of Israel.*

v. 13: *Then you shall know that I am the Lord, when I open your graves, and when I raise you from your graves, O my people[a],*

v. 14: *and I will put my spirit within you and you shall live, and I will place you in your land and you shall know that I, the Lord have spoken and will do it, says the Lord.[a]*

3.8.2. Text Critical Notes

v. 11 [a] LXX expands the subject with κυριος. Thus, "the Lord said."

v. 11 [b] Some manuscripts add ו before הנה – "and behold." The original Greek reading runs as: "and they," omitting הנה. Targum and Vulgate also read "and they" perhaps presupposing a personal pronoun. Driver proposes to read as הנה and placing המה after it.[289] Block asserts that this is the only instance in which the quotation is introduced with. הנה [290] The particle serves two functions in this context. Rhetorically it represents a quasi-interpretive attention-getter. Logically, it provides a link teaming up with לכן in v. 12 to create an occasion-response, if not cause-effect sequence of clauses. Thus the MT reading needs no emendation.

---

[289] Cited by Zimmerli, *Ezekiel 2*, 256.

[290] Block, *The Book of Ezekiel 25-48*, 182.

v. 11 [c] With 37 manuscripts including LXX and Targum delete "ו" before אבדה (and it will perish). Therefore, it should be deleted, and thus having a perfect meaning "perished."

v. 11 [d-d] "we are cut down" is proposed to emend with נגזר נולכו– "our thread of life has been cut off." However, Zimmerli argues that the language and imagery of this reading is attested nowhere else in the Old Testament,[291] so, the proposal should be declined.

v. 12 [a] The MT reading עליהם (unto them) is absent in the LXX. But may not need deletion because the message received by the prophet concerns the people, who are in exile.

v. 12 [b] אדני is absent in the original Greek reading. According to Zimmerli, the expression אדני יהוה (the Lord God) is really characteristic of the book of Ezekiel. In the book the divine name occurs in this expanded form for 217 times.[292] Thus, it is to be retained.

v. 12 [c] The MT reading of עמי is unrepresentative in LXX and Syriac. It probably originated as comparative gloss on לעם "to people" in the verbal covenant formulation of v. 27. The context needs not the phrase because the sentence already shows the address. As Cooke suggests,[293] it should be omitted from the context.

v. 13 [a] עמי is omitted by Syriac but retained in LXX. The LXX may retain it by dittography from v. 12. Allen argues that its presence in the LXX may indicate that it was first incorporated into the text at this point and subsequently entered in v. 12 by assimilation.[294]

v. 14 [a] Syriac reads, "says the Lord God" – The usage of אדני יהוה (the Lord God) is frequently found in the book of Ezekiel. However, the emendation is not necessary here.

3.8.3. Form Critical Notes

Ezekiel 37 is broadly divided into two equal parts, viz, Vision of dry bones (vv. 1-14) and, the oracle of the Two Sticks (vv. 15-28).

---

[291] Zimmerli, *Ezekiel 2*, 256.

[292] See additional notes on "The Divine Name in the Book of Ezekiel" by Zimmerli, See *Ezekiel 2*, 556ff.

[293] See Cooke, *The Book of Ezekiel: ICC*, 400.

[294] Allen, *Ezekiel 20-48: WBC*, 183.

Scholars are in the opinion that the first section is composed of two separate sections, vv. 1-10 and vv. 11-14, thus stand in a relationship of image and interpretation.[295] Thus the unit vv. 1-14 is called in various ways: The resurrection of Yahweh's people (Block), The resurrection of dead Israel (Zimmerli), Restoration of Life for Israel (Cooper), The promise of New Life (Allen), etc. Interpretation of the vision of dry bones (vv. 11-14) or may be called as "an interpretative oracle of salvation" (Allen) is cast as a continuous divine speech, framed by a new address of the prophet, בן־אדם (mortal/human one) at the beginning, and the signatory formula at the end (נאם אדני יהוה) The image of dry bones (1-10) is replaced by that of the graves (vv. 12-13). The section is opened with a thesis of despair (v. 11), and a counter thesis of hope (vv. 12-14). Thus v. 11 begins with a quotation of the words of the people, which is followed by the divine response in vv. 12-14.

The genre of the unit is what is called a disputation speech consisting of a thesis of despair and a counter thesis of hope.[296] It is a disputation speech, opening with a quotation of popular opinion (v. 11), followed by a refutation (vv. 12-14). The refutation itself is a complex, sub-divided into two parts (vv. 12-13 and 14), each of which contains a promise of divine action and an expanded recognition formula. The vision of dry bones is expanded in this section in which reconstruction of the body and the revival of the still dead body by the spirit are the main themes. The promise of restoration is culminated in the giving of the Spirit of God upon them so that the people would realize God's purpose in his act.

There is a general consensus that the occasion for the vision and its interpretation is the hopeless situation of the exiles. Wevers dates the passage from the period after 586 BCE, but considerably before chapter 36.[297] Allen also agrees that there can be little doubt that this unit reflects a situation not long after 587 when sentiments

[295] For these structural divisions, most of the scholars agree with each one another. However, the form of the two units is attested in which vv. 1-10 is the vision account and vv. 11-14 is its interpretation. For more detail see Allen, *Ezekiel 20-48: WBC*, 183; Zimmerli, *Ezekiel 2*, 257., and Wevers, *Ezekiel*, 278.

[296] Allen, *Ezekiel 20-48: WBC*, 183.

[297] Wevers, *Ezekiel*, 277.

of death-like hopelessness occasioned by the shock of Jerusalem's fall, the dissolution of Judah and the Babylonian exile must have been rife.[298] While some have argued for redactional activities, most commentators believe that the prophecy could not be very far from the original author, the prophet.[299] Therefore, the prophecy is the polemic formulation of restoration of the exiles. Thus, with the dating of the section, in spite of the suggestion of certain elements of Ezekiel's later language (v.2a) it is better not to go too far into the exilic period.

3.8.4. Comments in Relation to the Meaning and Significance of the Spirit of God

The above passage, which may be called "an interpretative vision of Ezekiel," is God's response to the people's expression of hopelessness. The promise of new life or restoration is preceded by a statement of hopeless situation of the exiles with three metaphors: 1) bones – which stands for whole person, sapped of vitality; 2) dead – dead-like state (dried up bones); and 3) loss of life (literally cut off). According to Hals, "can these bones live?" was designed to show the impotence of Israel during the exile and the bones refer to the whole house of Israel.[300] In all three quotations (v. 11), full expression is given to lamenting the hopeless "fading, dying, being cut down." To this hopelessness, the prophet is delivering the divine proclamation. First Yahweh is opening the graves, lead his people out of the graves, and bring them into the land of Israel (v.12-13a). This will be accomplished by the bestowal of the Spirit of God by which people will live (v. 14a).

---

[298] Allen, *Ezekiel 20-48: WBC*, 184.

[299] Bertholet, Fohrer, and Wevers assign 12b-13 as a redactional insertion, John and Hermann regards vv. 13b-14 as redactional. However, analysis of its form and theme suggest extreme proximity to the genuine words of Ezekiel and a response to the fall of Jerusalem. Thus, the authenticity is defended. See discussion in this regard in Zimmerli, *Ezekiel 2*, 257. Allen, *Ezekiel 20-48: WBC*, 184.

[300] Cited by Cooper, *Ezekiel: NAC*, 324. Human bones can be mentioned as representatives of the whole person in the Old Testament in many instances. See Pss. 31:11; 38:10; Prov. 17:22; etc.

The historical act of Yahweh's liberating his people is culminated in the transfer of the land (v.14b), which will, however, be possible with the bestowal of the Spirit of God. It is possible because the Spirit of God will make them alive.[301] In the larger context of vision of dry bones (vv. 1-14) we encounter in eight instances the use of the term "spirit," having different connotations.[302] While a newly bestowed spirit of life is emphasized in the preceding verses, the reference here is explicitly to "my spirit," that is the Spirit of God. Thus one must think beyond the mere reification of the promise of the spirit in 36:27, by which also the inner transformation of the people comes about. Cooper thus comments that the message and encouragement of the prophet will produce a life transforming experience that would result in national resurrection.[303]

What will be the exact implication of raising up of the dead and the enlivening of the people in this passage is a matter of debate. According to Lang, this passage actually implies a version of resurrection belief. The hope involved not only restoration of Israel, but also the new Jewish commonwealth with some of the dead.[304] Some of the Rabbinic teachings witness different implications.[305] If we look in to the situation of the exiles and prophetic response, there is no doubt to say that the primary concern of this vision would be the revival of the nation of Israel. It is the Spirit of God that enlivens the dead, which also binds the community together and gives it the will to live and accept its future.[306] Thus, the Spirit of God (will be

---

[301] Zimmerli, *Ezekiel 2*, 263.

[302] In vv. 1 and 14 Spirit of God is referred to. In v. 5, 6, 8, 9 (twice), and 10 "breath" is implied. Either in the form of air, breath or spirit, the energizing force of life as the influence of God is emphasized.

[303] Cooper, *Ezekiel: NAC*, 325.

[304] Bernhard Lang, "Life after Death in the Prophetic Promise," *Supplement to Vetus Testamentum, Congress Volume: Jerusalem 1986*, edited by J.A. Emerton (Leiden: E.J. Brill, 1988), 154f.

[305] For Rabbi Elleazer, it implies post-exilic Israel, for Rabbi Judah ben Bathrya, it implies the Ephramites. See detailed discussion in Block, *The Book of Ezekiel 25-48*, 387f.

[306] Blenkinsopp, *Ezekiel*, 173.

put upon you) plays a role of giving life to the lifeless exiles so that restoration would be achieved.

3.9. Permanent Gift of the Spirit of God

3.9.1. Text: Ezekiel 39:25-29

v. 25: Therefore thus says the Lord[a] God: Now I will restore[b] the fortunes of Jacob and I will have mercy the upon[c] the house of Israel; and I will be jealous to my holy name.

v. 26: And they shall forget[a] their shame and all their faithlessness with which they were unfaithful unto me; when they dwelt securely in their land and no on terrifies (them),

v. 27: when I bring them back from the people I will gather them from the lands of their enemies, and through them I will be honoured before the sight of [a]many nations[a].

v. 28: Then they shall know that I am the Lord their God [a]who sent them into exile[a] among the nation and I will gather them into their own land, I will leave them again no more.

v. 29: And I will no longer[a] hide my face from them, when I have poured out my spirit[b] upon the house of Israel, says the Lord God.

3.9.2. Text Critical Notes

v. 25 [a] As in the previous passages אדני is employed here which is absent in the original Greek reading. Since it is the characteristic of Ezekiel to use אדני יהוה, it should be retained.

v. 25 [b] Many manuscripts found at Cairo Geniza follow the qere, that is שׁבוּת.

v. 25 [c] על is used here instead of the MT כל, which is not attested by the LXX and Latin version. Two manuscripts read על "upon." Looking at the context, the emendation is likely.

v. 26 [a] Few manuscripts and certain ancient versions retain the MT with a long form "ונשׂאו" – and they shall bear.[307] Hitzig's proposal to read ונשו "and they shall forget" is adopted by BHS, RSV, NEB and NJB. Zimmerli denies the emendation stating that the verb never occurs in Ezekiel and the phrase נשא כלמה occurs very frequently in

---

[307] Se Allen, *Ezekiel 20-48: WBC*, 202.

Ezekiel other than the single term.[308] Wevers taking the MT reading interprets that the exiles "will bear their shame" means that they will remember their sins during the coming age as perpetual warning, on the one hand, and recognise God's mercy on the other.[309] Hitzig's proposal is agreeable since a statement of salvation is expected here.

v. 27 [a-a] הגוים רבים (many nations) is unusual and ungrammatical, as רבים is not expected here. LXX omitted the adjective. However, Syriac, Talmud, and Vulgate retain this. Allen and Zimmerli consider הגוים to be original and רבים to be a comparative gloss relating to 38:23.[310] Since nations could be interpreted in a collective sense in the OT, the omission is possible.

v. 28 [a-a] בהגלותי literally means "I who to take into captive" (ב +Hiph. Inf. +Suff. Ics. גלה – to take into captive).[311] The LXX takes a niphal form (I who uncover myself/reveal myself), but this is contradictory to the point of view of the subject matter; the aim of which is to guarantee Yahweh's righteousness. Deportation occurs because they sinned before God. Therefore, the MT reading is theologically sound.

v. 29 [a] עוד is lacking in certain Greek versions as well as in Syriac. The flow of the passage is still meaningful.

v. 29 [b] The LXX has tonv qumon mou (my wrath) to refer to Yahweh's anger. Vulgate has "*spiritum meum*" – to refer to "spirit that brings salvation." The Greek reading seems to be an exegetical interpretation.[312] Therefore, the MT reading is more appropriate in this context.

3.9.3. Form Critical Notes

Ezekiel 39:25-29 is the last section of what is called the Oracles against Gog, running through chapters 38-39. This two chapters form a unit of oracle as introduced by the introductory formula, "The word of the Lord came to me saying" in 38:1, and closed by a

---

[308] Zimmerli, *Ezekiel 2*, 295.

[309] Wevers, *Ezekiel*, 295.

[310] See Allen, *Ezekiel 20-48: WBC*, 202, Zimmerli, *Ezekiel 2*, 295.

[311] See Brown Driver Briggs, *Lexicon*, 163.

[312] Allen, *Ezekiel 20-48: WBC*, 202. Cf. Isa. 59:19; Zech 6:8; Prov. 16:19.

signatory formula, "says the Lord God" in 39:29. The unit vv. 25-29 is one of the several oracles within the two chapters characterized by distinctive forms.[313] Thus, there is no unanimity in relation to the pericope of each unit.[314] The unit 39:25-29 is one of the oracles introduced by an introductory formula לכן כה אמר אדני והוה. The sevenfold division introduced by the formula are: 38:3-9, 10-13, 14-16, 17-23; 39:1-16, 17-24, and 25-29. There have been various views concerning the beginning of the pericope for what is considered the concluding section of the Gog oracle. Block identifies vv. 21-29 as the epilogue of Gog oracle and is a late expansionic modification.[315] However, Block as well as Eichrodt, Wevers, Smend, and Hermann identify the unity of vv. 25-29 as the conclusion for the oracles of 36-37 and the Gog oracle of 38-39.[316] The pericope of the unit is marked by an introduction formula כח אמר אדני והוה and concluded with the formula לכן נום אדני יהוה (Thus says the Lord God). The unit may be structured as: the actions of Yahweh (v. 25); the response towards God's action (v. 26-27); the recognition of Yahweh by the people (v. 28); and the outpouring of the Spirit of God (v. 29).

With regard to the genre of the oracle, there have been diverse views. F. Hitzig was the first to assign the oracle of Gog as "apocalyptic," claiming that it does display features associated with

---

[313] The pericope of each unit is not easy to demarcate because of complexity of each unit in terms of signatory formula, introductory formula, and messenger formula found in the passage elsewhere. For example, Purnak finds four-fold division introduced by signatory formula; Wevers finds eight conclusion formulas marking eight-fold division. Taylor and Smart have seven separate oracles introduced by a introduction formula. Seed detail in Allen, *Ezekiel 20-48: WBC*, 202. Wevers, Ezekiel, 285. Zimmerli, *Ezekiel 2*, 296.

[314] One has to note that the occurrences of different formulas could not altogether agree with the structures based on theological themes.

[315] Daniel I. Block, "God and the Pouring out of the Spirit: Reflections on Ezekiel XXXIX 21-29," *Vetus Testamentum* 37 (1987): 265. Zimmerli, Holscher and Cooke also advocate the end of Gog oracle in v. 20 and see vv. 21-29 as the concluding section added by a later redactor. See Cooke, *The Book of Ezekiel: ICC*, 421f., Zimmerli, *Ezekiel 2*, 298.

[316] See Block, "Gog and the Pouring Out of the Spirit," 265, Wevers, *Ezekiel*, 285, and Eichrodt, *Ezekiel*, 521.

later apocalyptic literature.[317] Block, Darr and Collins, who even though recognize apocalyptic features in the oracle, choose to call it "prophetic eschatology."[318] The passage in this unit represents prophetic proclamation of restoration of the exiles in the future and hence the feature of prophetic eschatology is the genre of the pericope.

The section of the epilogue (vv. 21-29 or particularly vv. 25-29) represents a characteristic feature which marks it off from the main oracle of Gog. However, the links between them could not be overlooked.[319] Therefore, the setting of the unit could be traced in the light of the Gog oracle, or at least they are interrelated. To sketch the tradition-history of the Gog oracle and identification of the name Gog and Magog along with the explanation of the hordes of Gog are extremely difficult. There have been various attempts to deal with this problem, but there is no satisfactory solution for the problem.[320] Davidson takes it as the embodiment of the idea of irreconcilable hostility of the nations of the world to the religion of Jehovah.[321] For Cooper, the tradition is a symbol of Babylon.[322] Stalker argues that the tradition may now be lost, but is used as a material to produce

---

[317] Cited by Ktheryn Frizterer Darr, "The Book of Ezekiel," 1513. Also advocated by P.L. Redilt, Ahroni, and Cooper. See Cooper, *Ezekiel: NAC*, 328.

[318] According to Hanson, Prophetic Eschatology is different from Apocalyptic Eschatology that the latter being largely an outgrowth of the former. Prophetic Eschatology is a religious perspective which focuses on the prophetic announcement to the nation of the divine plans for Israel and the world. Cited by Darr, "The Book of Ezekiel," 1514.

[319] For example, the description of Israel in v. 27 appears to contain a deliberate summing up of the state of the nation at the time of Gog's invasion as described in 38:8, 11.

[320] Some have argued that Gog is to be identified as one of the nations in the Ancient Near East as referred in the table of the nations in Gen. 10:2. Some others identify it with Gyges, the Lydian king (ca. 660 BCE), or to the apocalyptic synonym for the Babylonians, Scythians, Old Testament antichrist, Alexander the Great, Gagu-a city prince, and so on. See more detail in Zimmerli, *Ezekiel 2*, 301f., Block, *The Book of Ezekiel 25-48*, 433f.

[321] A.B. Davidson, *The Book of the Prophet Ezekiel* (Cambridge: Cambridge Univ. Press, 1892), 274.

[322] Cooper, *Ezekiel: NAC*, 332.

Ezekiel 38-39.[323] When and where is the Gog oracle produced in its original form is quite important, but hard to ascertain. There are two opposing views: the first school views that it was Ezekiel himself who composed the oracle.[324] The other school represented by Holscher, Ewald, Hermann, Torrey, Allen and others deny the authorship of Ezekiel basing on a nuance of redactions in the passage.[325] The moderate view represented by Zimmerli advocates that the basic text is in no way stylistically different from what is usual elsewhere in Ezekiel, but rather corresponds to that.[326]

It is most probably possible when scholars attribute the basic core to Ezekiel and the subsequent layers to his school. Therefore, basing on its similarity of styles, it may be right to advocate that the oracle is original to the prophet and that the concluding parts such as vv. 25-29 may be a later date. The setting of the unit could therefore, be later than the prophet himself.

3.9.4. Comments in Relation to the Meaning and Significance of the Spirit of God

The impacts of Yahweh's saving activity is portrayed and sealed by a promise of change with the style of prophetic eschatology in this section. The passage not only concludes the Gog oracle, but also provides the purpose of God's choice of the exiles in his act of restoration. God's choice of Israel and restoration is for the gathering of the house of Israel who will know that Yahweh is their God who pours out his spirit upon them as a seal of covenant relationship. Because of divine judgment the spectral manifestation of Gog has vanished, to be replaced by the imminent change in Israel's destiny. This will be accomplished by the assembling of the exiles who will be a new people of God upon whom God's jealousy is shown.

---

323 Stalker, *Ezekiel*, 261.

324 This is the traditional understanding of authorship of the oracle still advocated by Block and others.

325 This school advocates a work of later redactor mostly in the post-exilic period. For example, Torrey assigns the third century use of Babylonian mythology for the oracle. See Torrey, *Pseudo-Ezekiel*, 96.

326 See Zimmeri, *Ezekiel 2*, 302.

The outpouring of the Spirit of God, however, serves as a guarantor of divine favour and of the future unbroken fellowship between God and his people.[327] Block here observes a more surprising twist; a stereotypical threat of judgment שָׁפַךְ חֲמָתִי (I will pour out my wrath) overturned to שָׁפַךְ רוּחִי (I will pour out my spirit).[328] Block asserts that the conjunction in verse 29 (אֲשֶׁר) clearly links the permanence of the new relationship described in v. 29a with the pouring out of the Spirit of God upon the house of Israel in 29b.[329] The communication of the Spirit of God is described as the final irrevocable union of Yahweh with his people (cf. Joel 2:29), and is associated with the messianic age of a future prospect.

What is the significance of "pouring the divine spirit upon the house of Israel?" Block suggests that it signifies the ratification and sealing of the covenant relationship, more than this, it signifies the definitive act whereby Yahweh claimed and sealed the newly gathered nation of Israel to his own.[330] Thus, it signifies the gift of God for new life, peace and prosperity to the whole house of Israel. It should be distinguished from "the giving (נָתַן) of the spirit in 36:27, and the "to put my spirit within (בְּקֶרֶב) of 38:27. The phrase "pour out my spirit upon" is found in other prophetic writings.[331] The poured out of Spirit of God serves as a permanent seal of the eternal covenant, which is also mentioned in 37:26. A "new thing" preached by Deutero-Isaiah and a "new covenant" of Jeremiah is realized with the gift of Yahweh's enabling Spirit. In short, the long, dark period during which Yahweh's face remained hidden has now come to an end with the outpouring of the Spirit.

In this final episode of the Oracle, Ezekiel concludes that Yahweh redeemed his people so that the house of Israel affirms his greatness, holiness and glory. This is made possible only because

---

[327] Eichrodt, *Ezekiel*, 529.

[328] Cf. Ezek. 7:8; 9:8; 20:8, 13, 32, 34; 30:15; 36:18.

[329] Block, *The Book of Ezekiel 25-48*, 488.

[330] Block, "Gog and the Pouring out of Spirit," 269.

[331] Cf. Joel 3:1; Zech. 12:10; Isa. 32:15; 44:1-5. In these passages the renewal of the covenant and the restoration of prophecy and peace for Israel are mainly emphasized.

Yahweh fulfilled his covenant to his people by pouring his *spirit* (Spirit) upon them. The presence of the Spirit of God poured upon the returned exiles guaranteed that he would never leave the house of Israel at the mercy of her enemies, and that he would never hide his face from them again. Therefore, the Spirit of God is an enabling power, which prepares the whole house of Israel for continuing life.

3.10. Summary

From the above study one can assume that the book of Ezekiel is a theological reflection on the exiles of the 6th century BCE. The prophecy, though received redactional elements, witnesses original words of the prophet of the exile as shown by its characteristic features. The prophet who lived and active during that time challenged the exiles to have faith in Yahweh. One of the theological interests of the prophecy to be seen is the characteristic use of spirit and the Spirit of God. These usages have significant meanings and significances for the prophet as well as for the exilic community. The foregoing exegetical studies show that the Spirit of God in the book of Ezekiel is the divine power operated in various ways. First, the text in 3:12-15 suggests that the Spirit of God is a moving force, which is responsible for displacement of the prophet in his visionary experiences. Second, the exegetical study of 11:4-6 indicates that the Spirit of God is not only a moving force; it is an inspiring force that prepared the prophet for prophecy. Here, the tradition of Ezekiel moved beyond the existing tradition of the prophecy, which denies inspiration by the Spirit of God. In 36:24-28 we encounter a specific role of the Spirit of God whose role is described as transformation of the people.

The significance of the Spirit of God is that it prepares the exiles by enabling inward change so that God would deliver them from their captivity. The Spirit of God plays a role of restoring people from the countries of their enemies as the Spirit of God gives life to the lifeless exiles. This is expressed in 37: 11-14. Finally, the Spirit of God is not only "given" or "put within," but also poured upon the house of Israel, which marks the permanent endowment of the Spirit of God to the house of Israel. Ezekiel 39:24-29 represents prophetic eschatology in which God's renewal and fulfillment of the covenant promise to the exiles is explicitly demonstrated that God would never leave his people any more. The Spirit of God in the book of Ezekiel, therefore, is the gift of God, the divine empowering influence upon the prophet and restoring power for the exiles, so that they may become the people of God.

Chapter 4

The Meaning and Significance of the Spirit of God in the Book of Deutero-Isaiah

4.1. Introduction

The book of Isaiah chapters 40-55 is generally taken as a unit, popularly known as Deutero-Isaiah or Second Isaiah. There are numerous themes reflecting different theological issues in the book. The book has been interpreted as a response to the situations of the exiles. Thus, it demands serious inquiry as different theological understandings are shaped in this period. One of the theological interests seen in this book is about the Spirit of God. The prophecy witnesses a specific use of the Spirit of God with varied meanings and significations. Therefore, this chapter deals with the study of the meaning and significance of the Spirit of God in the book by exegeting relevant passages. A brief introductory statement on authorship and composition of the book is looked upon, which is followed by a brief survey of the use of Spirit of God. The main study is exegesis of three selected passages, which are considered to represent the use of the Spirit of God in Deutero-Isaiah.

4.2. The Book of Deutero-Isaiah: Authorship and Composition

The book of Isaiah chapters 40-55 has been considered the work of an unknown prophet/prophets called Deutero-Isaiah or Second Isaiah. The prophet is distinguished from the author of Isaiah 1-39 as demonstrated by great difference in their historical background and literary characters.[332] The unit is considered to be a response to a kind of disillusionment among the exiles about their faith and refutations of the claims of Babylonian religion, which comes from the exiles of Babylonia shortly before the dawn of Persian Empire (550-540).[333] It was Duhm who first distinguished Third Isaiah (56-66) from chapters 40-55, which however, attains serious criticisms.[334] In spite of criticisms, it is a general consensus that Deutero-Isaiah forms a distinct unit in terms of themes and content.

Regarding the authorship, the book does not provide biographical information. Even though some scholars try to find the author's name from the text, the author is still anonymous. C.R. North argues that the hint of author's name in 42:19 where משלם ("dedicated one" or a personal name Meshullam) is in opposition to "the servant of Yahweh."[335] Few hints we can gain about the author from his work indicate that he was himself one of the Jewish exiles in Babylonia, possibly the one born in Babylon, of a family exiled from Palestine. According to Torrey, Second Isaiah was a philosopher and

---

[332] This is demonstrated by the fact that the prophecy of 1-39 deals with historical situations of Assyrian period whereas 40-55 speaks at the end of Babylonian exile, reflecting the period of Babylonians and the Persian king Cyrus. See discussion in Reuben Levy, *Deutero-Isaiah: A Commentary* (London: Humphrey Milford, 1925), 1.

[333] E.W. Heaton, *The Old Testament Prophets* (London: Darton, Longman & Todd, 1977), 107.

[334] Duhm's thesis is challenged on various grounds: (a) each section of the prophecy is considered to have undergone successive redactions; (b) its unity with the other sections (1-39 and 55-66) in terms of thematic and structural unity is affirmed, and (c) also the place of writing could possibly be Palestine. See discussion in Joseph Blenkinsopp, *A History of Prophecy in Israel,* revised and enlarged (Louisville, Kentucky: Westminster John Knox Press, 1996), 185ff.

[335] C.R. North, *The Suffering Servant in Deutero-Isaiah* (Oxford: Oxford University Press, 1959), 184.

poet who lived in the fifth century BCE.[336] While later collection and preservation of Deutero-Isaiah's original work is accepted, the main body of the book is attributed to the prophet himself, who lived in the sixth century.[337]

Regarding the date and place of writing, Torrey claims that there is not a word in Deutero-Isaiah which could be said to point plainly to Babylonia as the place of its composition.[338] There are, however, considerable supports for the exilic date and Babylonian context for the place of writing in the text.[339] The main thesis for this is that the coming of Cyrus is anticipated in the passages and that a kind of polemic against Babylonian religion is suggested in many of the references.[340] Therefore, basing on these evidences, scholars conclude that the prophecy comes from the late exilic age, possibly by about 550-540 BCE.[341]

In recent years, there have been strong criticisms concerning the tripartite division of the book of Isaiah. One of the issues that contributed to the debate is separation of the servant songs in Deutero-Isaiah, which for some scholars are later than Deutero-

---

[336] Cited by James D. Smart, *History and Theology in Second Isaiah: A Commentary on Isaiah 35, 40-66* (Philadelphia: The Westminster Press, MCMLXV), 18.

[337] This is advocated by Westermann, Smart, C. R. North, etc. See detail in Claus Westermann, *Isaiah 40-66: A Commentary* (London: SCM Press Ltd., 1969), 29.

[338] Charles Cutler Torrey, *The Second Isaiah: A New Interpretation* (Edinburgh: T & T Clark, 1928), 20f. According to Torrey, references to Babylon and Chaldeans, the mention of Cyrus, etc are later interpolations.

[339] From the text, one can infer that the release from Babylon is still in the future (55:12f.), the advance of Cyrus is alluded (41:1ff), and the Diaspora to the four winds (nations) is attested – which indicates a sufficient time after the fall. There are enormous polemic tendencies against Babylonian religion in the book. See detailed discussions in C.R. North, *The Second Isaiah: Introduction, Translation and Commentary to Chapters XL-LV* (Oxford: Clarendon Press, 1964), xl-lv., Smart, *History and Theology in Second Isaiah*, 32.

[340] See 45:20-25; 46:1-2; 47:1-15.

[341] Thus advocated by McKenzie, Holladay, North, etc., See J.L. McKenzie, *Second Isaiah: Anchor Bible* (New York: Doubleday & Company Ltd., 1968), xviii.., William L. Holladay, *Isaiah Scroll of a Prophetic Heritage* (Grand Rapids, Michigan: Eerdmans, 1978), 16. Also See North, *The Second Isaiah*, 4.

Isaiah.[342] Another issue of the debate is the structural divisions in 40-55, which is broadly divided into 40-48 and 49-55.[343] Thus Keunen, Kosters and Kittel believe that 49-55 were written or delivered in Palestine immediately after the return. Another debatable issue with regard to the composition is the issue of unity of Isaiah (1-66). This claim proposes that the book as a whole is a literary unit, united by a common structure that is the context for making sense of the book's individual parts.[344] There are various theories proposed by Old Testament scholars regarding the unity of the book of Isaiah.[345] The emphasis on the unity of Isaiah 1-39 with that of 40-55 (40-66), therefore, does not go back to unity of authorship, but to recurring vocabulary, themes, and editing mechanisms uniting the book.[346] The two sections 1-39 and 40-66 may be related to each other, but written in different contexts.[347] Critical look at the contents and structures could not undermine isolated historical situations and distinct theological interests, and thus one cannot deny the possibility of different authorship and composition for Isaiah 40-55. Therefore, Isaiah 40-55 will be taken as the second book of Isaiah

---

[342] Duhm in 1892 was the first to isolate and give a title "Servant Songs" to the four group of passages viz:- 42:1-4; 49:1-6; 50:4-9, and 52:13-53:12. See McKenzie, *Second Isaiah*, xxxviiiff.

[343] 40-48 is concerned with one main theme - that is the sovereignty of God, with the servant Cyrus as Yahweh's anointed one. Chaps. 49-55 does not have any reference to Cyrus and no more emphasis on the sovereignty of God. Important themes are Zion and the people of God with words of exhortations. See Levy, *Deutero-Isaiah A Commentary,* 9ff.

[344] David Carr, "Reaching For Unity of Isaiah" *JSOT* 57 (March, 1993): 64.

[345] For example, Childs affirms the unity in terms of canonical unity. See B.S. Childs, *Introduction to the Old Testament as Scriptures* (Philadelphia: Fortress Press, 1979), 325ff. Clements sets the historical context of 587 as the centre of the whole prophecy that calls forth the prophecy of judgment (1-39), promise (40-55), and a carrying forward of divine words to the post- exilic community (56-66). See R. E. Clements, "Beyond Tradition-History: Deutero-Isaianic Development of First Isaiah's Themes" *JSOT* 31 (February, 1985), 94.

[346] Richard J. Clifford, "The Unity of the Book of Isaiah and Its Cosmogonic Language," *CBQ* 55/1 (January, 1993): 1.

[347] John N. Osswalt, *The Book of Isaiah Chapters 40-66: NICOT* (Grand Rapids: Michigan: Eerdmans, 1998), 6.

or Deutero-Isaiah written by the unknown prophet/prophets of the late exilic period.

4.3. The Spirit of God in Deutero-Isaiah

The term *ruah* occurs in eleven instances in the book of Deutero-Isaiah, which could be translated in various ways including, wind, breath, and spirit.[348] In some instances it is used in relation to the dynamic force - a natural force as wind (41:16). Sometimes, it is used to refer to inner faculty of human kind (54:6). In some instances the term signifies nothingness (41:16). In most of the cases spirit is used in relation to God as "power manifested from God" (40:7; 42:5). Moreover, spirit is the gift of God (42:5; 44:3). Above all, the term "spirit" in relation to God may be used to refer to personality of God or the divine nature of God (40:13; 48:16). The exact phrase "Spirit of God" is found in two instances (40:7 & 40:13). But the term "my spirit" (רוחי) is found in two places (42:1 & 44:3); and "his *spirit*" (רוחו) is found in 48:16. Thus spirit and Spirit of God is used in the book in various contexts, having various meanings and significations. Therefore, we will look at the book of Deutero-Isaiah to delineate the meaning and significance of the Spirit of God by exegeting relevant passages.

4.4. The Spirit of God and Establishment of Justice

4.4.1. Text: Isaiah 42:1-4

v. 1: *Behold[a] here is my servant whom I uphold, my chosen one[a], in whom my soul delights; I have put my spirit upon him; he will bringforth justice[b] to the nations.*

v. 2: *He will not cry out[a] nor lift up[b] his voice; he will not make it heard in the street;*

v. 3: *[a]The crushed reed he will not break[a]; and a dimly burning wick he will not extinguish[b]; [c]he will faithfully[c] bring forth justice.*

v. 4: *He will not grow faint[a] or be crushed[b], until he establish justice on the earth; and the coastlands shall wait for his instruction.*

---

[348] NRSV translates the term as spirit in 40:13; 42:1; 42:5; 44:3; 48:16; & 54:6; as breath in 40:7 & 42:5; and as wind in 41:16 & 41:29.

4.4.2. Text Critical Notes

v.1 [a-a]The demonstrative particle or interjection הן is usually translated as behold/lo. The primary function of הן according to Labuschagne is to call attention to something or some person.[349] Thus its use in this context presupposes that the servant is introduced to a group. Instead of הן עבדי LXX inserts Jakob, before "my servant" and Israel before "my chosen one" to have metrically smooth in arrangement so that it will be parallel to 41:1; 42:1; 44:1. Thus the MT presupposes Israel to be the servant of the Lord. Targum renders the word תמך as קרב (draw near) thus translates as "behold my servant, I will bring him near." Torrey takes עבדי (my servant) and בחירי (whom I choose) as collocation which refer to Israel, as seen in 41:8,9; 43:10; 44:1; 28.[350]

v. 1 [b] Qumran Scroll of Isaiah (DSS [Isa]) adds ו in both ends to mean, "and his justice/judgment." LXX, Vulgate and Syriac support the MT. The term has been translated differently. Vulgate chooses "judgment." Westermann and Whybray follow RSV, which translates as "justice."[351] Thus, we will be translate as "justice"

v. 2 [a] DS[Isa] renders as יזעק. But the verb form of זעק is not used. The emendation is unlikely.

v. 2 [b]The literal meaning "to lift up" necessitates the object קול. Targum has יכלי (to cry aloud). Thus, some have argued to translate as "cry out" as justified by Num. 14:1.[352] Cheyne and others emend to ישאג (he will roar).[353] The MT needs no emendation because קול נשא is a well known Hebrew Idiom (Cf. Isa. 3:7; Num 14:1; Jer 1:17; Mic. 6:9, etc.).

---

[349] Cited in Daniel Jones Muthunayagom, *The Relationship Between Election and Israel's Attitude Towards the Nations in the Book of Isaiah* (Delhi: ISPCK, 2000), 101.

[350] Torrey, *The Second Isaiah*, 325.

[351] See Claus Westermann, *Isaiah 40-66: A Commentary* (London: SCM Press Ltd., 1969), 92. Also R.N. Whybray, *Isaiah 40-66: NCB*, edited by R.E. Clements (London: Oliphants, 1975), 72.

[352] So Muthunayagom translates it. See *The Relationship Between Election and Israel's Attitude*, 102.

[353] Cited by Torrey, *The Second Isaiah*, 325.

v. 3 [a-a] Targum has "the humble who are like the bruised reed." This is rather an added comment as the same interpretation is seen in the next colon: "the dimly burning wick he will not..."

v. 3 [b] The MT יכבנה literally means "he will quench it." DSS[Isa] has יכבה without suffix which means "he will shatter." This is perhaps the original rendering.

v. 3[c] לאמת (literally "to truth") has been translated differently. Kittel's *Biblia Hebraica* renders as לאמות "to the peoples."[354] LXX renders as αλλα εις αληθειαν "but in truth." Griesbrect reads לאמות "to the nations."[355] Peshitta has בקשתא (in the task, certainly), RSV renders as adverb, "He will faithfully bring out justice." NIV takes it as substantive, "In faithfulness." The translation is implied by the treatment of the term as adverb of substantive. אמת comes from אמן, and it underlines the fact that the servant will execute all that has been said in the preceding verse. It thus portrays a sense of certainty and firmness in the performance of the servant's mission.[356]

v. 4 [a] יכהה literally means "burn dimly." LXX renders as αναλαμψει (he shall shine out). RSV and KJV renders, "fail" Targum has יהלי – "to be tired." The RSV, "grow faint" is plain.

v.4 [b] The literal meaning of ירוץ is "he will break." LXX reads: "he will be broken," Targum: "He will become tired," and Syriac: *ntptq* "he is extinguished." Based on the LXX, BHS suggests a niphal form "be crushed." Thus, the emendation is to be retained.

4.4.3. Form Critical Notes

There are various views expressed by commentators with regard to the pericope of the unit. The most widely accepted view after Duhm is that Isaiah 42:1-4 is a unit in itself with its specific characteristics. This view regards Isa. 42:1-5 as the first of the four servant songs.[357] The second view is that Isa. 42:1-9 is a literary composition which is a

---

[354] See Rudolph Kittel (ed), *Biblia Hebraica* (3rd edn.), (Stuttgart: Wurttembergische Bibelanstaltt, 1937).

[355] See as quoted by Levy, *Deutero-Isaiah*, 145.

[356] See discussion in Muthunayagom, *The Relationship Between Election and Israel's Attitude*, 103.

[357] The others being 49:1-6; 50:4-9; and 52:13-53:12. Duhm assigns a later date for these songs. But it is believed that they do not point to different authorship,

combination of two seemingly identical units.[358] Though some have treated vv.1-9 as a unit, the demarcation within the unit, 1-4 and 5-9 is well established as shown by change of address.[359] Therefore, as suggested by a number of scholars, vv. 1-4 will be taken as a unit, which may be called as "The servant of Yahweh – his endowment and mission."[360] The unit is introduced by a demonstrative particle הִן which is a popular term in Deutero-Isaiah. The end of the unit in verse 4 is attested by an introductory formula in verse 5, "Thus says the Lord God" (כֹּה־אָמַר הָאֵל יְהוָה). These verses describe the election, endowment and mission of the servant. God's creative and liberative power "Spirit of God" is endowed upon the servant so that he would accomplish his mission. The unit may be structured as follows: a) Presentation of the servant as Yahweh's elect and equipment of the servant with the Spirit of God (v. 1), b) Manner of the execution of the mission (v. 2-3); and c) Assurance of the execution of the mission.

The structure, form and content of the passage show that the poem is characterized by an anointment of a king for specific tasks. Paul E. Dion who finds parallel texts with ancient appointment ceremony of the kings ascribes the genre "appointment of kings to the throne," to the unit.[361] The identification of the servant in the poem is varying from one to another. Some identifies it as the prophet himself (Whybray), or a representative figure of Israel (K. Koch). The servant is most probably to be identified as a royal

---

nor are they distinct from the rest in terms of language and thoughts. See McKenzie, *Second Isaiah: Anchor Bible*, 37. Also See, Whybray, *Isaiah 40-66: NCB*, 70.

358 This view is advocated by K. Koch, K. Baltzer, P.E. Dion, H. C. Spykerboer, K. Kida, Metinger, O Kaiser, Carlos Mesters, and others. Though these scholars treat 42:1-9 as a unit, their methods and their conclusions regarding the identity of the servant and the nature of the servant's tasks vary considerably from each other. See detailed discussion in Muthunayagom, *The Relationship Between Election and Israel's Attitude*, 107.

359 Thus vv. 1-4 addresses the servant (he), vv. 5-9 to the second person (you)

360 North, Westermann, McKenzie, Levy, Skinner, Whybray, Wade, Herbert, G.A.F Knight, and others support this view.

361 Paul E. Dion, " Institutional Model and Poetic Creation, the First Song of the Servant of the Lord and Appointment Ceremonies" in *Ascribe to the Lord*, edited by Lyle E., Eliner & Glenn Taylor (Sheffield: JSOT Press, 1988), 319ff.

figure as shown by the nature and mission of the servant.[362] The ANE parallels and the semantic parallels in the other parts of the Old Testament also witnessed to the royal figure.[363] Therefore, the unit envisages a royal figure upon whom the Spirit of God would be endowed to establish justice upon all the earth.

With regard to the setting of the unit, there is a widely accepted view that it is authentic to Deutero-Isaiah.[364] While the exact historical background is not clear, the contents of the unit point to the exilic situations. For example, the metaphorical use of a dimly burning wick (v. 3) suggests the lifeless situation of the exiles. On the other hand, "to bring forth justice" (vv. 1&4) implies the anticipation of the removal of oppressive conditions of the Israelites. According to Lindblom, the figure of the servant in 42:1-4 is delineated against the background of the victorious and triumphant Cyrus.[365] The setting of the prophecy might possibly be the dawn of restoration, after the rise of Cyrus, probably about 540 BCE, the time when Media was already at the hand of Cyrus, and restoration of Israel was yet to achieve.

4.4.4. Comments in Relation to the Meaning and Significance of the Spirit of God

The so-called the first servant song (42:1-4) speaks about two important themes which can be portrayed from the verses. Firstly it talks about the election and equipment of the servant. Yahweh's addressing the servant as "my servant" indicates the intimate relationship in which the servant is dependent on Yahweh.[366]

---

[362] The nature and mission of the prophet points to a kingly figure who will judge the nations, by establishing justice to the nations.

[363] Cf. Isa 11:1-5; Ps. 72:1-4; I Sam. 16: 1-13; II Sam 3:18. For discussion of the ANE parallels see Muthunayagom, *The Relationship Between Election and Israel's Attitude*, 108f.

[364] Whybray, *Isaiah 40-66: NCB*, 71.

[365] Joh Lindblom, *The Servant Songs in Deutero-Isaiah* (Lund: CWK Glerup, 1951), 18.

[366] In the Old Testament we encounter the use of עבד יהוה with reference to a number of persons like Abraham, Moses, David, etc. Thus the term is used in connection with God's election of persons for his purpose.

Moreover, "my chosen one" signifies that the choice of the servant is a deliberate act, and a purposeful choice. The next statement further expresses the election, "whom I uphold, my chosen, in whom my soul delights." The election of the servant is confirmed by the guaranteeing of the Spirit of God.

We note that the Spirit is the charismatic impulse which moves men (sic.) to deeds of strength, courage and wisdom.[367] Here, the phrase נתתי רוחי עליו is used in parallel to 11:2 which expresses the endowment of the Spirit of God to the anticipated royal child which equips him to defend the true *mishpat* (משפת). Earlier rulers of Israel also received the gift of God's spirit to empower them to perform special tasks (Judg. 6:34; I Sam 10:10; I Sam 11:2). Hanson enunciated that through the empowerment of the Spirit of God, weak and ordinary human beings rise up to accomplish daunting tasks on behalf of God's reign of justice.[368] What will then be the meaning of putting the Spirit of God upon the servant? It means that God guarantees that the way of the servant will be effective and that God is always in control.[369] It means that the task of the servant can be accomplished only by divine power.[370] It may presuppose the permanent endowment of the Spirit of God upon the servant to involve himself unceasingly to the execution of Yahweh's purpose. The passage thus shows that the mission of the servant is possible only with the operation of the Spirit of God, which will enable to establish משפת on earth.

Secondly, the unit contains a very important issue concerning the nature of the mission and the manner of its execution. The gift of the Spirit of God to the servant is for the establishment of משפת (vv. 1c, 3c, ad 4b). Scholars are not in the same opinion to the meaning and interpretation of משפת and the concern expressed by

[367] See discussion in McKenzie, *Second Isaiah: Anchor Bible*, 36.

[368] Paul D. Hanson, *Isaiah 40-66: Interpretation*, edited by James Luther Mays et.al. (Louisville: Westminister John Knox Press, 1995), 44.

[369] G.A.F. Knight, *Deutero-Isaiah: A Theological Commentary on Isaiah 40-55* (New York: Abingdon Press, 1965), 73f.

[370] A.S. Herbert, *The Book of the Prophet Isaiah Chapters 40-66* (Cambridge: Cambridge Univ. Press, 1917), 40.

Deutero-Isaiah towards the nations through this statement.[371] The term משפת is a word for many meanings, but it may probably be assumed that it has the same meaning in the three places of this unit. In Israel's tradition, keeping משפת and preservation of the rights of the marginalized and the oppressed is the primary task of the king (II Sam. 8:15; Deut. 33:21; Ps. 7:12; 72:1-3; Isa. 1:17 etc.). Yahweh constantly creates new משפת for the oppressed (Pss. 9:9; 12:2; Zeph. 3:5). Thus, the Hebrew משפת is much more than judicial equity. In its broadest sense, it involves societal order in which the concerns of all are addressed.[372] Therefore, It is that life-giving order which exhibits when the creation is functioning in accordance with the reign of its Lord.

Verses 2-4 portrays the manner of the servant's execution of the mission. This is portrayed in a form of negatives: "he shall not cry, nor lift up, nor make it to hear" (v.2).[373] This statement is further explained in v. 3 by metaphors "he will not break a crush reed, nor will he not quench a dimly burning wick." North explained that both figures imply that the servant will never despair to even the most abandoned outcast.[374] Thus, the proclamation of the rule of God would be a comfort to the exiles who were lifeless and stayed in a crisis situation. The manner of execution of the mission is concluded with the proclamation that the servant will establish משפת upon the earth (v. 4). Thus the mission of the servant is to be accomplished with establishment of justice on earth. Therefore, we may conclude that the Spirit of God is the equipment of the servant who in the time of

---

[371] Rowley interprets this statement that Israel has to bring to all people the true religion. For Snaith it means justice in the sense of strict retribution to the nations. For Zimmerli it is a realization of Israel's right and its international affairs to the nations. For Beuken, it means redemption of Israel from Babylonians and Israel's movement towards Zion. See Muthunayagom, *The Relationship Between Election and Israel's Attitude*, 110f.

[372] Osswalt, *The Book of Isaiah Chapters 40-66: NICOT*, 110.

[373] Volz, Fohrer and Elinger interpret the negatives as contrast between the servant's functions and those of earlier prophets of doom. Cited by Whybray, See *Isaiah 40-66: NCB*, 72.

[374] North, *The Second Isaiah: Introduction, Translation and Commentary*, 109.

Israel's darkest days will serve the task of liberating and establishing justice, not only in Israel, but also to the ends of the earth.

4.5. The Spirit of God and Eschatological Hope

4.5.1. Text Isaiah 44:1-5

v. 1: But now[a] *hear, O Jacob my servant; Israel whom I have chosen;*

v. 2: Thus says the Lord who made you, and who formed you [a]*in the womb*[a]*; he will help you; Do not fear, O Jacob my servant, Jeshurun*[b] *whom I have chosen;*

v. 3: For I will pour out water on a thirsty land[a]*, and streams*[b] *upon the dry ground; I will pour out my spirit*[c] *upon your descendants, and my blessing upon your offspring.*

v. 4: And they shall spring up like [a]*grass in the midst of water*[a]*, like poplars by flowing streams.*

v. 5: This one will say, " I am the Lord's; and another will be called[a] *by the name of Jacob; and this one will write on his hand*[b]*, "Belonging to the Lord," and will be called*[c] *by the name of Israel.*

4.5.2. Text Critical Notes

v. 1 [a] ועתה is a clause which connects the previous passage either as a connection or as contrast. According to Osswalt the clause refers to a logical sequence rather than a temporal one, thus to be translated as "and now."[375] In line with this, Whybray believes that the clause does not refer back to the previous passage but to an unrecorded lamentation to which this oracle is a reply.[376] Skinner translates it "yet now" marking the contrast.[377] It is more likely to render as "but now" since the previous passage (43:22-25) speaks of Israel's past and this new section contrasts the past sin of Israel with salvation oracle.

v. 2 [a-a] According to Stuhlmueller מבטן must be joined to the preceding ישראל to mean "I have made you from the womb"[378] The

---

[375] Osswalt, *The Book of Isaiah Chapters 40-66: NICOT*, 164.

[376] Whybray, *Isaiah 40-66: NCB*, 82.

[377] J. Skinner, *The Book of the Prophet Isaiah Chapters XL-LXVI* (Cambridge: Cambridge Univ. Press, 1917), 51.

[378] Carroll Stuhlmueller, *Creative Redemption in Deutero-Isaiah* (Rome: Biblical Institute Press, 1970), 125.

preposition מִן here has the locative meaning "in" as attested in the Ugaritic reading. Thus the rendering "in the womb" is retained.

v. 2 [b] LXX, Peshitta, Syriac, Targum, and some manuscripts read ישראל instead of Jeshurun. But they were interpreting the MT. This is evident in the LXX where the expansive statement is attested as: "Israel the beloved." Vulgate adds: "Israel most virtuous," and other Greek reading has: "Israel the honest." The term occurs again in Deut 32:15; 33:5, 26; always as a synonym for Israel and a title for honour. The origin of the word is obscure, but most scholars connect it with ישר "upright."[379] Wade argues that the term may be translated as "upright/straight" to point to the contrast with the name Jacob.[380] It may also be a play on the word "Israel."[381] The form Jueshurun is similar to Jeduthun and Jebulun where "un" ון is to be taken as diminutive.[382] Since the exact meaning of the term is obscure to retain it, "Jeshurun" as the MT may be sound.

v. 3 [a] The adjectival form of צמא means "thirsty" or "a thirsty one." BHS suggests to read as צְמָא a noun "thirst" as also seen in Syriac and Targum. To add "land/ground" makes sense.

v. 3 [b] צמא is translated in LXX as "the one passing by" which may be a confusion with אזל "to go/go about" The participial form of נזל means, "to flow," "to trickle," or "to drop." Thus RSV renders as "streams."

v. 3 [c] Instead of רוחי the Targum of Isaiah reads as "my holy spirit"[383] This may not be implied here. The preceding colon "blessing" is used in its original sense of vitality of power which bestows fertility. Therefore, the use of רוחי is meaningful in the contexts.

---

[379] See Levy, *Deutero-Isaiah*, 169.

[380] G.W. Wade, *The Book of the Prophet Isaiah* (London: Methuen & Co. Ltd., 1929), 284.

[381] Torrey advocates that on account of metrical ground the play on word is seen here as Israel and Jeshurun. See Torrey, *The Second Isaiah*, 344.

[382] Diminutive are often used to express affection. Thus "beloved." See A.E. Cowley, *Gesenius' Hebrew Grammar*, Edited and Enlarged by E. Kautsch (Oxford: Clarendon Press 1910), 240.

[383] See J.F. Stenning (ed & trans), *The Targum of Isaiah* (Oxford: Clarendon Press, 1949), 148.

v. 4 [a-a]נזלים (literally among/between grass/trees) is considered to be a corrupt reading. So, suggestion is to read as: אזל (like grass amidst waters). LXX, Qumran Scroll, and Targum read so. RSV follows LXX as: "like grass amidst waters" Another significance for חצור in cognate Semitic roots suggests that it refers to a kind of a tree. חצור (grass) is proposed to emend as Hazor- a royal city of northern Canaan; which may not be implied here. The LXX may be retained in this context.

v. 5 [a]The MT יקרא in an active sense (he shall call) is supported by the LXX. But one manuscript suggests a passive klhqhsetai "will be called." Syriac, Targum, and Vulgate support the MT. Levy reads, "This one shall call himself by Jacob's name."[384] However, many recent interpreters prefer the passive sense יקרא since the object is lacking.[385] Thus, the passive "will be called" is probably the appropriate reading.

v. 5 [b] wdy (his hand) is emended by LXX, Greek Symachus and Athanasius readings, and Latin Vulgate as "in/by his hand" or the sense is "on his hand." Thus, it is supposed that ב is omitted by haplography.[386] It is best to take "his hand" as accusative and to add b to it.

v. 5 [c] יכנה (he will call/title) is a Piel imperfect form of כנה. The rendering assumes the emendation יְכֻנֶּה or יְכַנֶּה for the received יכנה. Since it lacks an objective, passive or the reflexive is more likely. Targum and Vulgate thus have passive. The cognate verb in Arabic *kunya* is a surname or a heroic title, or a household name.[387] Therefore, the best reading would be a Pual "be titled" or "be called."

4.5.3. Form Critical Notes

Most of the scholars agree with the unit of the passage 44:1-5, which is generally called as a salvation oracle. While few scholars[388] find no

---

[384] Levy, *Deutero-Isaiah*, 170.

[385] Cited by Watts, *Isaiah 34-66: WBC* Vol. 25, edited by David Hubbard et. al., (Waco, Texas: Word Books Publisher, 1987), 140. Among the scholars, Torrey objects to the passive reading. See *The Second Isaiah*, 344.

[386] North, *The Second Isaiah: Introduction, Translation and Commentary*, 134.

[387] See more detail in Skinner, *The Book of the Prophet Isaiah Chapters XL-LXVI*, 52.

[388] Among those advocates Watts and Smart are well known figures.

break between chaps. 43 & 44, majority of the exegetes argue that the opening ועתה (44:1) emphasizes the relation of contrast between what has been said in the previous verses.[389] Thus, it functions as an opening of the unit. The end of the pericope is again demonstrated by a new formulaic introductory כה אמר יהוה in verse 6. Thus Isaiah 44:1-5 bears the characteristics of a self-contained oracle of salvation. However, the unit is connected with the preceding trial speech of 43:22-28. Therefore, Osswalt is right when he says that the unit stands apart because it contrasts what has been already said about Israel's condition in 43: 22-28.[390] Seitz also finds in this passage, the transition from transgression of the past to God's new action in the present.[391] The unit may be structured as: God's continued love and election (vv. 1-2), the promise of outpouring of the Spirit of God upon the house of Israel (v. 3-4), and the privilege of foreigners in the days to come (v. 5).

With regard to the genre of the unit, it is generally agreed that the passage is an oracle of salvation belonging to the general type characterized by the formula אל תירא (do not fear).[392] Some have argued that the unit is distinct from ordinary salvation oracle as suggested by eschatological nuances. Westermann asserts that the cry "fear not" is followed by one in the form of future tense. The promise of salvation is assurance of salvation; not promised to the recipients of this oracle, but to their descendants.[393] Watts on the other hand

---

[389] Scholars such as Osswalt, Whybray, McKenzie, Paul D. Hanson and others advocate this stand.

[390] Osswalt, *The Book of Isaiah Chapters 40-66: NICOT*, 164.

[391] Seitz, however refers 43:22-25 as words of transgression and 44:1-7 as discussion of God's new action in the present. See Christopher R. Seitz, "The Book of Isaiah" *New Interpreter's Bible*, Vol. VI, edited by Leander E. Keck et. al. (Nashville: Abingdon Press, 2001), 385.

[392] According to Stuhlmueller, oracles of salvation are seen as individual poems in Isaiah in the following: 41:8-13; 41:17-26; 43:1-7; 43:14-15; 43:16-21; 44:1-5; 46:9-13; 54:4-6; 54:7-10. See Stutuhlmuller, *Creative Redemption in Deutero-Isaiah*, 17.

[393] Westermann, *Isaiah 40-66*, 134.

finds announcement of judicial decision as the main tenet of the oracle, and hence he classifies it as decree of judicial decision.[394]

It is the promise of brilliant future, and eschatological hope. Therefore, one may rightly find the Gatung in this passage, that is, an eschatological hope of salvation. The oracular formulae: "hear," "thus says the Lord," "and fear not," refer to a strong note of authority intended to arouse in the audience to listen to the voice of God. This is further strengthened by the characteristic clauses, "my chosen" "my servant." These features suggest a salvation oracle. Moreover, the oracle of salvation in this passage is differing from general salvation oracle that it refers mainly to a more remote future. Thus, this oracle is a promise that the nation will survive and multiply even as God's spirit will be poured upon them in the coming days.

The setting of the unit is most probably the exile of Babylonia at the dawn of restoration. According to Watts, the passage encourages the exiles who were confronted by the advance of the idols from the cities as well as the armies of Medo-Persian.[395] Seitz argues that the image of trees/grass is more than general wisdom reflection, but rather serves as a contrast to deforestation of Assyria.[396] The assurance of salvation with characteristic clauses suggests the approaching confident hope of restoration. The universal aspects of the oracle, "one will say I am the Lord's... another will be called by the name of Jacob, one will be called by the name Israel (v. 5)," suggest tolerance and universalism of Deutero-Isaiah. Even though the exact date is not clear, the passage is possibly an outcome of the late exilic age where the exiles are challenged to witness the saving power of Yahweh among the nations.

4.5.4. Comments in Relation to the Meaning and Significance of the Spirit of God

The oracle of salvation or eschatological hope of salvation in this passage is introduced with the word ועתה in contrast to what was

[394] Watts, *Isaiah 34-66: WBC*, 143.

[395] Watts, *Isaiah 34-66: WBC*, 143f.

[396] Cf. Ps 1:3; Isa. 10:28-11:9. See detailed discussion in Seitz, "The Book of Isaiah," 380.

said of Israel's past in 43:22-28. Once more the election of Israel is confirmed by two designations: "my servant" and "my chosen." The same two verbs "make and form" again reiterate the election, which also point to salvation.[397] The election and assurance of salvation is further supplemented by the phrase "who help you," (v.2) which implies election of Israel among the nations. The theme of election is strongly affirmed by the formula אל תירא which is a form of speech, which indicates assurance of salvation. The designation of Israel/ Jacob here is ישורון which is used to refer to Israel elsewhere. Thus, the danger of extinction of the exiles is contrasted that Israel is in the hand of God who creates, helps and chooses her.

The assurance of salvation is not only for the exiles, but also for their descendants. Moreover, the promise of eschatological hope of salvation is given to the exiles that the Spirit of God will be poured upon the descendants of Israel (v. 3). Metaphors are employed here to illustrate the proclamation of salvation. "Pouring on a thirsty land and flowing streams on the dry ground" speaks of new day when God will do the impossible for his people, when he will turn death to life.[398] There are varying interpretations for the meaning of "pouring out the Spirit of God upon your descendants." For Duhm, Volz, and Muilenburg it signifies a new beginning for the Israelites as a result of Cyrus' advance.[399] Smart believes that it talks about the eschatological hope projecting the future.[400] The oracle is a promise of salvation in contrast to the previous statement of destruction, and that the pouring out of the *spirit* upon the descendants will, therefore, points to restoration and continued presence of God with

---

[397] The same two verbs occur in the creation stories of Genesis. North argues that according to Genesis all previous history had been a preparation for the calling of Israel; and thus creation and forming of Israel would mean saving action of God. See North, *The Second Isaiah: Introduction, Translation and Commentary*, 132.

[398] See image of water in a dry land in Isa. 12:3; 30:25; 32:2; 33:21; 35:6; 41:18; 43:20; 51:3; 45:1; 66:12.

[399] Cited by Smart, *History and Theology in Second Isaiah*, 111. See also James Muilenberg, "The Book of Isaiah Chapters 40-66: Introduction and Exegesis," in *The Interpreter's Bible* Vol. V, edited by G.A. Buttrick et.al. (New York: Abingdon Press, 1956), 502.

[400] Smart, *History and Theology in Second Isaiah*, 111.

Israel. One has to make a note on the parallel usage of pouring the spirit and blessing. Westermann defines the parallel reference to mean the giving of vitality or power of God, which bestows fertility of the land.[401] The dry ground being transformed is that of Israel itself, and that Yahweh's spirit will be poured upon... signifies that it will cause restoration, and salvation of the future generation.

The last verse of the unit describes that when the Spirit of God is poured upon the offspring of Israel, Gentiles will also enjoy the goodness of it. Scholars are not in the same opinion regarding the interpretation of verse 5. While some deny any hint of universalism, some have argued that the phrase represents the beginning of universalism.[402] McKenzie interprets that the prophet here predicts that foreign peoples and nations also will be impressed by the saving power of Yahweh that they will take his name and the name of his people.[403] It is likely that the oracle predicts a day when, because of the work of the Spirit of God among his people, the awaited salvation of Israel will be achieved and people of all sorts will enjoy the goodness of it. One may conclude that the Spirit of God poured upon the descendants of Israel signifies future restoration and salvation of Israel, which will also be benefited by all sorts of peoples.

4.6. The Spirit of God and Prophetic Proclamation

4.6.1. Text: Isaiah 48:16

v. 16: *Draw near to me, hear this; from the beginning*[a] *I have not spoken in secret,* [b]*from the time it was,*[b] *there I am.* [c]*And now* [c] *the Lord God* [d] [e]*sent me and his spirit* [f]*.*

---

[401] Westermann, *Isaiah 40-66*, 136.

[402] For Volz, Duhm, and North it points to the converts of Gentiles to Yahwism, and for Osswalt there is nothing about universalism in the passage, as Israel knows nothing of a mission to the Gentiles. But for many exegetes, including Smart, Herbert, Knight, McKenzie, and others, it points to universalism. See discussions in George A. F. Knight, *Deutero-Isaiah: A Theological Commentary*, 113., A.S. Herbert, *The Book of the Prophet Isaiah Chapters 40-66*, 57., North, *The Second Isaiah: Introduction, Translation and Commentary*, 134., Osswalt, *The Book of Isaiah Chapters 40-66: NICOT*, 168.

[403] McKenzie, *Second Isaiah: Anchor Bible*, 64.

4.6.2. Text Critical Notes

v. 16 [a] מראשׁ (from the beginning) literally "from the earliest form or from the head." Its actual implication is obscure. It probably points to events long past (cf. 8:3-5; 40:21; 41:4). According to Torrey, the Assyrian *ulturesi* is used in the same way to refer to long past.[404]

v.16 [b-b] מעת היתה is literally to be translated as "from the time it became." RSV and NRSV render as "From the time it came to be..." McKenzie puts it: "from the time it happened." Stuhlmueller renders as: "From the time it started happening." North makes a note that here מִן is marking the *terminus a quo*.[405] Precisely what the third person feminine suffix "its" refers to is not indicated. The translation, "from the time it was" is a probable reading since the events described points to past actions.

16 [c-c] ועתה (and now) is a technical term used frequently by Deutero-Isaiah (48:14). Depending on the context, it could be both "and now" and "but now." It is used to relate the two parts of the statements. It shows that the two parts are clearly connected in form and content. Knight acknowledges that the term is a technical term specifically used by Deutero-Isaiah for the contemporary moment.[406] Here, it connects the former cola (about the former events) with the last cola which speaks of the sending of the prophet and his spirit.

16 [d] אדני יהוה is omitted by LXX and Arabic version. But DSS [Isa,] Targum, and Vulgate support the MT. Torrey and Levy take the use to be a gloss, whose original would be יהוה אלהים (the Lord God).[407] But the use is one of the characteristics of Deutero-Isaiah.

16 [f] רוחו (his *spirit*/spirit) is emended by Harvey as רוּחִי (my spirit/spirit) claiming that the same expression is found in the pattern of the Hittite suzerainty treaty in which the messenger bore an important place.[408] The preceding colon will clarify the meaning and usage of the term in this context.

---

[404] Torrey, *The Second Isaiah*, 378.

[405] North, *The Second Isaiah: Introduction, Translation and Commentary*, 181.

[406] Knight, *Deutero-Isaiah: A Theological Commentary*, 172.

[407] See Torrey, *The Second Isaiah*, 378. Also Levy, Levy, *Deutero-Isaiah*, 217.

[408] Cited by Stuhlmueller, *Creative Redemption in Deutero-Isaiah*, 158.

16 [e-f] שלחני ורוחו (sent me and his *spirit*) is a difficult line in this verse. Alt emends it as: "I sent him on his way (referring to Cyrus)"; and Volz, "I am his chosen one being sent" (taking בחירי instead of רוח.[409] There is a change of the speaker from third person (God) to the first person (sent me). Many exegetes propose that this line is a gloss and is to be omitted.[410] On the other hand, scholars such as Westermann, McKenzie, and Levy defend the authenticity of the last line as well as the verse.[411] The interpretation of the line is resulted by the attribution of רוחו "his spirit" whether as a subject or object. Normally in the Old Testament רוח does not send, but is always sent. Thus, to take as an object may be the most probable. Mc Kenzie's proposal that the line could be the imagined response of Cyrus to the commission is also likely.[412] Thus, the meaning of the line would probably runs as: "The Lord God sent me, and his spirit is also with me." Comments on the text may clarify the problem of its interpretation.

4.6.3. Form Critical Notes

Most interpreters divide Isaiah 48 into several poems, and this is recommended to some extent by diversity of topics and the ambiguity of the speakers. According to Duhm, a kind of consolatory poem of Deutero-Isaiah has been interpolated by a kind of interlinear commentary in which Israel's past is strongly condemned.[413] This is also the case in chapter 48. Commentators generally agree that the

---

[409] Cited by Muilenburg. See, "The Book of Isaiah" 561.

[410] Torrey proposes to omit the whole verse on the ground of meter and due to careless misinterpretation of the last line. Muilenburg argues that the term "his spirit" is awkward here and the line is a gloss. North, Wade, and Skinner suggest a later addition, possibly a work of Trito-Isaiah's circle. See Torrey, *The Second Isaiah*, 378., Muilenburg, "The Book of Isaiah" 561., North, *The Second Isaiah: Introduction, Translation and Commentary*, 182., and Skinner, *The Book of the Prophet Isaiah Chapters XL-LXVI*, 94.

[411] See Levy, *Deutero-Isaiah*, 217. McKenzie, *Second Isaiah: Anchor Bible*, 99., Westermann, *Isaiah 40-66*, 203.

[412] McKenzie, *Second Isaiah: Anchor Bible*, 99.

[413] Cited by North, *The Second Isaiah: Introduction, Translation and Commentary*, 175.

chapter consists of two major sections: vv. 1-11 and 12-22. Within these two major sections several minor units are acknowledged.

According to Laato, 48:16 is understood as standing apart from the main section vv. 12-22, which should be understood as a summary referring to the mission of the messenger of Yahweh.[414] It sums up the appeal of the previous four verses (vv. 12, 13, 14, 15), and is marked by another reference of a call קרבו אלי. Even though continuity or series of plea is acknowledged, commentators agree that there is a change of emphasis in v. 16.[415] New elements and distinctive nature of the verse is to be seen in ambiguity of the speaker and thematic break in the verse. The distinctiveness of the verse is again suggested by a new emphasis in v. 17 with an introductory formula, כה אמר יהוה. Therefore, we can detect change of the scene in v. 16 in spite of continuation of previous verses. The verse is composed of three cola. It can be structured as: a) A call to assemble (first colon). b) God has revealed himself at all time in Israelite history (second colon). c) Yahweh has sent the prophet as his *spirit* (last colon).

According to Whybray, the verse is to be understood in relation to vv. 1-12 which has the character of disputation in which Yahweh as the speaker seeks to overcome the exiles' doubts about the mission of Cyrus.[416] This verse thus argues the doubts of the exiles from the ground of Yahweh's limitless power and purpose already demonstrated in the creation of the world and the call of Israel. The disputation speech is introduced here with the imperative beginning in verse 1, שמעו־זאת (hear this), and a dialogue beginning in v. 16, קרבו אלי שמעו־זאת (draw near to me, hear this). Thus, the verse is a disputation speech with a dialogue defending the choice and mission of the prophet/Cyrus/Israel.

There has been debate as to the setting of the verse. The difficulty of tracing the setting of the verse and of the chapter is caused by possible work of a glossator and the ambiguity of the

---

[414] Antii Laato, *The Servant of Yahweh and Cyrus: A Reinterpretation of the Exilic Messianic Programme in Isaiah 40-55* (Stockholm: Almqvist & Wiksell International, 1992), 193.

[415] See McKenzie, *Second Isaiah: Anchor Bible*, 99., Watts, *Isaiah 34-66: WBC*, 178.

[416] Whybray, *Isaiah 40-66: NCB*, 130f.

speaker in the last line of v. 16. The interpretation of the speaker in the line largely effects scholars' attribution of the setting. For example, Volz attributes Cyrus as the speaker in this verse, and thus the setting would be the late exilic situation.[417] Watts finds a close connection of Yahweh and Cyrus in the chapter, and particularly in 16 and 20 where the expeditionary leader is depicted as ready to begin journey from Babylon to Jerusalem. He therefore, assigns a post-exilic dating in the period of Cyrus or Cambyses.[418] North believes that the verse is a later interpolation possibly by a member of Trito-Isaianic circle, who interjected the last line based on Isaiah 61:1.[419] Osswalt argues that the whole chapter addressed only to the exiles in Babylon and deals only with the promise of return.[420] It is probably a testimony of Yahweh's choice of Cyrus as liberator, which is intertwined with the prophet's statement of his initiation as the one proclaiming God's plan of salvation in this prophecy. Therefore, it is not necessarily a late-interpolation. One can suggest a late exilic age, at the dawn of restoration.

4.6.4. Comments in Relation to the Meaning and Significance of the Spirit of God

The lines of the verse though connected to each other contain two clear-cut emphases. Firstly the first and the middle lines are divine exhortation to Israel to hear that from the beginning he has not spoken in secret. He has been there in the midst of events of Israel's past. These two lines are interpreted in various ways. According to Wade, these lines talk about the election of Cyrus for his mission.[421]

---

[417] Cited by North, *The Second Isaiah: Introduction, Translation and Commentary*, 182.

[418] During this period, there were four expeditions that won poor support from the Jewish community, as reflected in Ezra-Nehemiah. See Watts, *Isaiah 34-66: WBC*, 176.

[419] North, *The Second Isaiah: Introduction, Translation and Commentary*, 182.

[420] See discussion in Osswalt, *The Book of Isaiah Chapters 40-66: NICOT*, 258f.

[421] According to Wade, "from the beginning..." implies from the very inception of Cyrus' enterprise against Babylon that the Lord's activity has been manifested in it. See *The Book of the Prophet Isaiah*, 311.

Kelly argues that it could be attributed to Yahweh who not only argues that he was present with the ancestors, but also with his word conveyed through the prophets.[422] Whybray comments that the argument of Yahweh's presence "from the beginning" is presumably intended to strengthen the argument concerning the reality of Cyrus' mission (cf. 45:19). Amidst different opinions, we may make a suggestion that these lines talk about the announcement of Yahweh's imminent presence in creation and his continued presence with the prophetic mission. The mission includes proclamation of Yahweh's choice and election of Cyrus.

When we come to the second line the problem arises primarily with the identity of the speaker and with his relationship with the speaker. While some have argued for a later interpolation, the authenticity of the line could also be maintained. As cited above, McKenzie believes it to be an imagined response of Cyrus to the commission. For Levy, it may well be the prophet's statement of his initiation.[423] The meaning of the line is implied by the interpretation of רוחו whether as subject or as an object. Taking as a subject, it signifies the person or being of God, as distinct from God. Therefore, spirit as the subject is to be denied. If taken as an object, what would be its implication? Kittel emends it, "I, Yahweh have sent him and his spirit."[424] Watts interprets thus: "someone, ostensibly a leader claims that Yahweh has sent him and his (God's) spirit."[425] Now, the scholarly debate on the identification of the speaker may be clarified as follows: The speaker here is the prophet, who had claimed that he was the one who in the dispute responds to the doubt of the exiles concerning the way of restoration. God sends the prophet himself, and the Spirit of God has filled him and thereby exhorts his compatriots to have faith in God and to him (the prophet). Thus, the verse speaks about the close identity between God and the prophet. God has been speaking through the prophet. He calls the people to

---

[422] Page H. Kelly, "Isaiah" *Broadman Bible Commentary* Vol. 5, edited by Clifton J. Allen et.al. (Nashville: Tennessee: Abingdon Press, 1971), 327.

[423] Levy, *Deutero-Isaiah*, 217.

[424] Cited by Smart, *History and Theology in Second Isaiah*, 149.

[425] Watts, *Isaiah 34-66: WBC*, 178.

listen because of all he (God) has said in the past, and now he (God) revealed himself in the events of their lives. Now, the prophet says, God is speaking again through me (the prophet) whom he (God) has inspired with his (God's) spirit. Thus, the Spirit of God is the empowering power of prophetic proclamation in the time of doubts and fears.

4.7. Summary

The above study shows that Isaiah 40-55, popularly known as Deutero-Isaiah reflects the theological issues in the context of doubts about Yahwism. In spite of disagreement on the authorship and composition of the book, it is generally agreed that the book comes from an unknown prophet of the late Babylonian exilic period, whose work shares considerable integration with that of Isaiah 1-39 and 56-66. One of the theological issues shaped by the crisis of the exile is that of the understanding of the Spirit of God. The phrase "Spirit of God" is not a very popular term, but has significant meaning for the exiles. This is demonstrated by its usage in the prophetic message. Exegetical studies of selected passages reveal that the term "spirit" either as "Spirit of God" or with suffixes, signify certain qualities of God in his acts of deliverance. Isaiah 42:1-4 portrays the Spirit of God as the agent of *mishpat*, through whom God establishes justice. It plays a role of establishing *mishpat* not only for the Israelites, but also for the whole earth. Isaiah 44:1-5 speaks about the pouring of the Spirit of God upon the descendants of Israel, which will also be benefited by the gentiles. This passage envisages that the Spirit of God is the saving power of God for the lifeless exiles. Moreover, it is the expected and awaited saving power of God for the future generation. Thus the Spirit of God is the divine power operating in the salvation of human kind, both now and in the future, not only for Israelites, but also for the Gentiles. With regard to 48:16, there has been continuing debate concerning its authenticity, especially on the last line of the verse. The verse describes that the work of God from the earliest continues till the events of the day. Moreover, the prophet makes clear that it is the same God who prepares the way of salvation through Cyrus, who is now speaking about the election of Cyrus through the prophet. In the context of doubts about the divine plan of salvation, the prophet claims that God sent him and God's spirit is also endowed upon him so that his proclamation is fair and true. Therefore, the Spirit of God is the divine empowering power, the authenticated word of God for prophetic proclamation.

Chapter 5

The Meaning and Significance of the Spirit of God in the Book of Jeremiah

5.1. Introduction

Prophecy of Jeremiah could be considered as one of the exilic prophetic literatures, for the assigned author was the one who first exercised prophetic ministry in the exilic age. The prophecy responds to the exilic age to prepare the exilic communities in the struggle for Yahwistic faith in the time of theological crisis. Even though the prophet does not directly express the term "Spirit of God," significant use of the term "*ruah*" in relation to God and parallel references to the Spirit of God are to be noted in the literature.

Scholars acknowledge impressive reasons for the absence of the phrase the "Spirit of God" in the book, and draw a conclusion that the book of Jeremiah shares similar theological outlook with that of other exilic prophets concerning the understanding of the Spirit of God. Therefore, the main discussion, in this chapter will be: a brief introduction to the book and the prophet, a study of the use of *ruah* in the book of Jeremiah, particularly in relation to God, an investigation of the prophetic conflict, usage of the "word of God" as parallel reference to the Spirit of God in Jeremiah, and exegesis of parallel reference to the Spirit of God in the selected passage.

5.2. The Book of Jeremiah: Authorship and Composition

The book of Jeremiah is considered to be a reflection and response to the historical crisis of the last days of Judah, culminating in the destruction of Jerusalem and the temple. The book is a complicated literary composition that has evoked much scholarly attention.[426] The shape of twentieth century scholarship on the formation of the book has been moulded by the pioneering work of Bernhard Duhm (1891) and Sigmund Mowinckel (1914).[427] Duhm proposes three source-theory which consists of: (1) the poems of Jeremiah (2) the narrative accounts of Baruch, and (3) the overlay of Deuteronomic theologians.[428] Mowinckel isolates four sources, each with its own redactor. He adds another source, (source D) which is found in chs. 30-31, which for him is a later collection attached to the book.[429]

In line with Mowinckel, Rudolph and Hyatt analyse the materials of different sources and assign redactional activities in compiling different sources.[430] For Nicholson, the book of Jeremiah has been reworked in order to be pertinent to the theological crisis of the exile, so that the book reflects the creative work of

---

[426] During the twentieth century, research on Jeremiah has focused on several issues such as the date of Jeremiah's call, his view of the Deuteronomic reform, the prophet's identification of the foe from the north, the differences between the MT and the LXX, and the composition and development of the book into its present canonical form. See more detail in Leo G. Purdue, "Jeremiah in Modern Research," in *A Prophet To The Nations Essays In Jeremiah Studies,* edited by Leo G. Purdue & Brian W. Kovacs (Winona Lake, Indiana: Eisenbrauns, 1984), 1.

[427] Cited in Robert P. Carroll, *Jeremiah* (Sheffield: JSOT Press, 1989), 32.

[428] Cited in Walter Brueggemann, *A Commentary on Jeremiah: Exile and Home Coming* (Grad Rapids, Michigan: Eerdmans, 1998), 7.

[429] Cited by Carroll. See Robert P. Carroll, *From Chaos to Covenant: Prophecy in the Book of Jeremiah* (New York: Crossroad, 1981), 261.

[430] Thus Hyatt assigns the Deuteronomic editors finished the major edition of the book around 550 BCE, perhaps in Egypt. See Leo G. Purdue, "Jeremiah in Modern Research," 15ff.

the generation.[431] Robert Carrol also advocates the Deuteronomic editing of the book.[432] Conservative critical position represented by Holladay and Bright, however, advocates authenticity of the book and argues that the materials do indeed stem from the work of the prophet.[433]

In spite of the fact that there is no consensus regarding the authorship and composition of the book, majority of the exegetes advocate a reworking of the original prophetic *verba impissa* in the exilic or postexilic age. Therefore, we will take the literature as a composite literature coming from both the prophet and the reworking of the redactor/s. In spite of possible redactional activity, the core of the prophecy is considered to be a respond to the historical situations of the exilic age of the sixth century BCE.

5.3. The Prophet and His Ministry

Jeremiah is the first known of the prophet who actually experienced the disaster of 587. Born from a priestly family at Anathoth, he received his call in the year 627/626 (Jer. 1:13f.).[434] His prophetic activity spanned forty years (627-587), from his call to the time

---

[431] Ernest. W. Nicholson, *Preaching to Exiles* (Oxford: Basil Blackwell, 1970), 14.

[432] Carroll writes, "It is the redactor's shaping of the confessions of Jeremiah, it is communities response to the tragedy, it is the laments of various sixth century groups, it is a later representation of the communities response to grief under the image of the prophet, or even a theologization of a divine suffering brought about by the destruction of the people. See Carroll, *From Chaos to Covenant*, 261.

[433] See William L. Holladay, *Jeremiah: Spokesman Out of Time* (Philadelphia: United Church, 1974) and John Bright, *Jeremiah: Anchor Bible* 21 (Garden City: Doubleday, 1978).

[434] According to Holladay, the fourteenth year of Josiah, 627 BCE (Jer. 1:2) is not the date of the prophetic call, but rather the date of his birth as suggested by no clear judgment for or against Josiah's reform in 622/621. Thus, 627 may probably be the date of his birth. William L. Holladay, "The Years of Jeremiah's Preaching" *Interpretation* XXXVII/2 (April, 1983): 147.

when he was taken to Egypt against his will (Jer.42-44).[435] We know almost nothing of Jeremiah's life during the reign of Josiah.[436]

Although we cannot be certain, it is possible that Jeremiah attacked the nation's harlotry, its worship of the Canaanite god, Baal, in the earliest years of his ministry, probably in the period immediately after his call in 627 BCE. The earliest datable record of his prophecy is found in the period of Jehoiachim in which Jeremiah proclaimed divine judgment upon Judah (26:1sff.). The king did not welcome this prophecy and now Jeremiah entered the most vigorous period.[437] During this time, the defeat of Egypt by Nebuchadnezzar (605 BCE) poised the invasion of Palestine itself. It was probably these events which prompted Jeremiah to compile a scroll of the oracles that he had hitherto utter and have them re-proclaimed as a unit in the temple by his scribe Baruch (cf. Ch. 36). The revolt of Jehoiachim against Babylonia and the consequent exile in 597 BCE prompted Jeremiah to proclaim divine judgment upon Judah and Syro-Palestine (13:11; 22:24-27; 38:1ff.). He also encouraged the group of exiles to settle down until their ultimate redemption from bondage (Ch. 29). He became increasingly the object of abuse at the hands of his countrymen during the reign of Zedekiah (597-587).

The outburst of those harsh treatments may be seen in the passages so-called "Confessions of Jeremiah."[438] After the fall of Jerusalem in 587 Jeremiah stayed with Gedaliah at Mizpah. A certain Ishmael assassinated Gedaliah. After these events, against his will, Jeremiah was taken to Egypt along with other deportees who were

---

[435] Bernhard W. Anderson, *Understanding the Old Testament* (New Jersey: Prentice-Hall, Inc., 1957), 326.

[436] There is only one short passage in the book explicitly dated in the reign of Josiah (3:6-11) and it is almost certainly not from Jeremiah but was composed by the Deuteronomistic authors to whom the book owes its present form. See detailed discussion in Nicholson, *Preaching to Exiles,* 3.

[437] In his Temple sermon Jeremiah condemned the popular belief of divine judgment upon the nation as temporary which had led the prophet to continuing conflicts with the king and professionals. See Ernest W. Nicholson, *The Book of the Prophet Jeremiah 26-52* (London: Cambridge Univ. Press, 1975), 6.

[438] The passages assigned to the confession are: 11:18-12:6; 15:10-18; 17:14-18; 18:19-23; 20:7-18. See discussion on the subject in Nicholson, *Jeremiah 26-52,* 1-10.

afraid of the reprisals from the Babylonians (42:7-22).[439] The last recorded episode of his ministry took place in Egypt and there, we may presume, he died. As one of the exilic prophets, the prophecy of Jeremiah responds to the great tragedy of the sixth century BCE in which profound theological thoughts are to be seen responding to the then situations.[440] The prophecy may be roughly outlined as:[441]

1) Prophecy and poems of Jeremiah (627-605) – Chapters 1-20.
2) Historical Narratives from the time of Jehoiakim and Zedekiah (605-587) – Chs. 21-36.
3) Events immediately prior to and following the fall of Jerusalem (587-ca.570) – 37-45.
4) Oracles against the nations – Chs. 46-51 and, 5) Historical appendix – Ch. 52.

5.4. The Use of *Ruah* in the Book of Jeremiah

While the exact phrase "Spirit of God" is not found in the book of Jeremiah, the term *ruah* occurs eighteen times having diverse meanings.[442] The term refers to ordinary word for wind or breath or

---

[439] See detailed study of the situations of the exiles in Egypt in the preceding chapter.

[440] Many scholars assign Jeremiah among the exilic prophets. See Ackroyd, *Exile and Restoration. Prophetic Voices in Exile.* (Philadelphia: Fortress Press, 1986); Thomas M. Raitt, *A Theology of Exiles* (Philadelphia: Fortress Press, 1977); Ralph W. Klein, *Israel in Exile, A Theological Interpretation.* (Philadelphia: Fortress Press, 1979); Walter Brueggemann, *Hopeful Imagination Prophetic Voices in Exile.* (Philadelphia: Fortress Press, 1986). Some others exclude Jeremiah because he was mainly active in the pre-exilic period (627-587), See Canon Shell, *Prophets of the Exile* (Madras: Diocesan Press, 1923); George Fohrer, *History of Israelite Religion*, translated by David E. Green (London: SPCK, 1972).

[441] S.K. Soderlund, "Book of Jeremiah" *ISBE* Vol. Two (E-Z), Edited by Geoffrey W Bromiley et. al., (Grand Rapids, Michigan: Eerdmans, 1988), 885. See also the same division with slight difference in Ernest Nicholson, *The Book of the Prophet Jeremiah 1-25*, 14-15.

[442] Albertz and Westermann, "רוח" *TLOT* Vol-3, edited by Ernst Jenni & Claus Westermann, translated by Mark E. Biddle (Massachusetts: Hendrickson Publishers, 1977), 1207.

spirit in some instances and refers to as the agent of God in most of the cases. Therefore, the Spirit of God is implied in some instances. Thus, it is significant to investigate different usage of *ruah* in the book of Jeremiah.

5.4.1. *Ruah* as Wind – God's Created Cosmic Power

One of the popular usages of *ruah* in the book of Jeremiah is with reference to wind- as the created cosmic power. In 10:13 & 51:16 we find "…he brings forth the wind (*ruah*) from his storehouse" and in 18:17, "… like the east wind I will scatter them…"13:24 also reads I will scatter you like chaff driven by the wind" These references speaks that the *ruah* is the powerfully created cosmic power operating in the direction of God. The oracle in 10:1-16 (cf. 51:16) asserts that in contrast to the stupid things (idols) Yahweh is the true creator of cosmic powers including heavens and earth, who brings forth lightning and *ruah* (wind) from his storehouse.[443] The רוח and קדים רוח of 13:24 and 18:17 signifies the power of the enemy who led the Judah into exile as the scattering before the wind, which is the judgment of God.[444] Thus, Judah will be scattered by the spirit as wind scatters the chaff. Whatever is the metaphor used, *ruah* in these texts refer to cosmic power which is in the control and direction of God.

5.4.2. *Ruah* as Breath - A Life-Giving Power of God

In two instances we encounter references to *ruah* as breath – a life-giving power. In 10:14 and 51:17 we find, "… there is no breath in them." In these two sections of the oracles, the emphasis is the power of the true God contrasted with the powerlessness of idols. In contrast to the Lord who sends forth his *ruah* (v. 13), the idols have no breath (*ruah*) in them.[445] The worshippers of idols are contrasted

---

[443] Carroll believes that a Babylonian or Persian background is assumed in this oracle that states the powers of cosmic beings. See Robert P. Carroll, *The Book of Jeremiah A Commentary* (Philadelphia: The Westminster Press, 1986), 258f.

[444] Brueggemann, *Exile and Home Coming*, 170.

[445] Thus it is called the breath (*ruah*) of God. See Peter C. Craigie, Page H. Kelly and Joel Drinkard Jr., *Jeremiah 1-25 WBC*, edited by David A. Hubbard et. al., (Dallas, Texas: Word Books Publisher, 1991), 160.

with the worshippers of the Lord. Breath (*ruah*) is the life-giving power because the images that are without breath (*ruah*) are fraud, senseless and worthless.[446] *Ruah* as breath signifies the dynamic life-giving power, which marks the presence of God in the living body.

5.4.3. *Ruah* as Four Compass Points

In a derived sense *ruah* is also used to refer to the four compass points. Here in 49:32 and 49:36 the usage is explicitly expressed in the idiom "the four winds."[447] Like the Akkadian "*sari erbetti*" the four corners of the earth reflects the hypothetical division of the earth into four quadrants. Accordingly, to be "scattered to the winds" (Jer. 49:32 Cf. Ezek. 12:14; 17:21) means to be dispersed in all the earth, the most severe exile imaginable.[448] The term *ruah* therefore has become a significant term in the exilic age to refer to the extent to which God's punishment will encompass.

5.4.4. *Ruah* as Nothingness

While *ruah* refers to cosmic power, the dynamic life-giving power and God's powerful agent, it also signifies nothingness or vanity in some instances. This expression is significant because it contrasts traditional understanding of the *ruah* (of God) by referring to the ineffectiveness of *ruah*. Thus 5:13 reads, "The prophets will become wind (*ruah*); the word is not in them." This verse is one of Jeremiah's attacks on the prophets who spoke falsely. Possibly there is a play on word that spirit (wind) of inspiration is lacking the divine word.[449] The verse is Jeremiah's own indignant rejoinder to the prophets who claim to have possessed the *ruah* to authenticate their prophecy.[450]

---

[446] F.B. Huey Jr., *Jeremiah and Lamentation: The New American Commentary* Vol. 16, edited by E. Ray Clandenen et.al., (Nashville, Tennessee: Broadman Press, 1993), 127.

[447] The oracle is about proclamation of judgment on Kedar and Hazor (vv. 28-32) and Elam (vv. 34-39).

[448] M.V. Van Pelt, W.C. Kaiser Jr., D.I. Block, "רוח," *NIDOTTE Vol.* Vol-3, edited by William A. van Gemeren et.al., (UK: Paternoster Press, 1996), 1074.

[449] Carroll, *The Book of Jeremiah*, 183.

[450] Cf. John Bright, *Jeremiah: The Anchor Bible* (Garden City, New York: Doubleday & Company Inc. 1965), 40.

Thus, Mowinckel writes: "for Jeremiah the *ruah (of)* men will become what in fact they always have been, namely "wind men," "nothing men."[451]

5.4.5. *Ruah* as Spirit/Wind – God's Agent of Judgment

Ruah is also portrayed as agent or instrument of judgment which is controlled and directed by God. The expression in 51:1 clearly portrays God's judgment in which *ruah* denotes destructive wind.[452] The rendering of *ruah* in 51:1 could be both wind and spirit.[453] Another reference to *ruah,* which signifies God's judgmental agent, is in 4:11&12. In this verses the rendering, "a hot wind... a wind too strong" signifies God's coming judgment which will not discriminate the good form the bad, but will engulf both alike.[454] While the *ruah* is dealing with "this people" and "my people," the judging agent of God is not a kind of wind which can be used for winnowing or cleansing. It is too fierce, too hot, and too oppressive to contribute positively to the life of the people. It is completely destructive; a hot wind is a metaphor for armies of invasion.[455] Thus the *ruah* (wind) comes at the behest of Yahweh, who now speaks about judgments against his people.

In addition to the usages of *ruah* mentioned above, there are few specific usages of the *ruah*. For example, in 14:6 and 2:24 where "sniffing the wind (*ruah*)" and "panting for air (*ruah*) like jackals," indicate *ruah* to mean air or necessary providential needs for livelihood. The absence of *ruah* (*spirit/breath*) is portrayed as

---

[451] Sigmund Mowinckel, "The Spirit and the Word in the Pre-exilic Reforming Prophets" *JBL* 53 (October, 1934): 206.

[452] The oracle is about judgment on Babylon in which *ruah* is portrayed as destroying power of God, an agent of judgment.

[453] Cf. east wind (sirocco) – Gen. 4:6; Job 15:2; Ps. 78:26; Isa. 27:8; etc.) While he translates as "a destroying wind," John Bright admits that the reference is of "the spirit" of a destroyer. See John Bright, *Jeremiah Anchor Bible*, 749.

[454] J. A. Thompson, *Jeremiah: NICOT* (Grand Rapids, Michigan: Eerdmans, 1980), 224.

[455] Carroll. *Jeremiah: A Commentary*, 163.

death for living animals.[456] There is also one reference (52:11), which speaks about "spirit" of the Median king as the agent of vengeance, which is described as God's appointed instrument for an eagerly awaited destruction of Babylonia.[457] Therefore, *ruah* in these passages described as breath, wind or spirit signify powerful-life-giving or destroying power, which is in the effect of God's authority and command.

5.5. Jeremiah and Prophetic Conflict

Owens writes, "A major part of Jeremiah's ministry was his attack on the professional religionist of his day."[458] From an early period of his ministry, Jeremiah had recognized the disastrous influence of the two professional religious orders in Jerusalem- the prophets and the priests. Of the priests as a separate body Jeremiah has not much more to say; but the prophets occupied much of his thought, and called forth his severest censure.[459] His conflict with the (false) prophets mainly deals with those who tend to support the political establishment and to speak assurances of peace based on present policy.[460] Jeremiah's polemic against the popular prophets of the time is mostly contained in a series of oracles delivered at various dates, and collected in Chaps. 23:9ff. under the heading לנבאים. The oracle is commenced with the striking expression "concerning the prophets…my heart is crushed within me… both prophet and priest are profane; even in my house I have found their wickedness, says the

[456] The passage talks about the drought in which the parched landscape with its dying creatures are seen in the destruction oracle. See Carroll, *Jeremiah: A Commentary*, 309f.

[457] This chapter is composed of a number of smaller units possibly composed before the dawn of restoration. See more detail in Huey, *Jeremiah and Lamentation*, 419.

[458] John Joseph Owens, "Jeremiah and the Cult" *Review and Expositor* LXVIII/3 (Summer, 1981): 373.

[459] J. Skinner, *Prophecy and Religion: Studies in the Life of Jeremiah* (Cambridge: Cambridge Univ. Press, 1930), 186.

[460] The clearest example is seen in exchange with Hannaniah in 27-28. See detailed discussion in Walter Brueggemann, "The Book of Jeremiah: Portrait of the Prophet" *Interpretation* XXXVII/2 (April 1983): 143.

Lord." (23:9-11). A great deal of space and attention is given to the prophetic message against false prophets. The prophecy mentions the falseness of the prophets or prophecy (4:9; 13:13; 23:1; 26:1f. 28:1); the sins of the prophets include "prophesying by Baal (2:8); they turned their back on Yahweh (2:27); they prophesy falsely (5:31; 6:13; 27:15-16). Prophetic conflict is dealt with in chapters 23, 26, 27 and 28 where professional religious leaders particularly prophets are condemned. They were called misleading shepherds because they were guilty of bypassing the source of true message (29:23b.). One of the factors that distinguished the true from the false prophets down from the pre-monarchic period is the inspiration by the Spirit of God.

Prophecy has been traditionally claimed to be associated with the Spirit of God.[461] Thus, Jeremiah's criticism of prophetic claims of his contemporaries is characterized by his view of inspiration. Jeremiah attacks prophets of the time as "not being sent by Yahweh" (23:18ff.), "the word of Yahweh is not in them" (5:13). "Their message was but a vision of their own mind" (23:16f.). "Prophets were stealing oracles from one another" (23:30). Thus for Jeremiah, those optimistic prophets were not inspired men of God as their claim of the Spirit of God is but only wind (5:13).[462] As the great classical prophets of the pre-exilic period did not speak possession of the Spirit of God in order to justify or authenticate their vision,[463]

---

[461] The inspiration of the *ruah* of God in the early period had a firm place in two contexts: (a) in the charismatic leadership and, (b) ecstatic prophecy. Thus the *ruah* of God is upon Joseph so that he could interpret dreams (Gen. 41:38). The J account of Moses' story is connected with both prophecy and ecstatic behaviour as the Spirit upon Moses was transferred to seventy (Num. 11:17-25). The same is true to the role of *ruah Elohim* upon Balaam whose influence is seen as ecstatic and prophetic in nature (Num. 24:2ff; 15).

[462] According to Mowinckel, this is known as the old Nebhi'ism in which prophetic inspiration was associated with ecstatic element, which was rejected by the reforming prophets of the pre-exilic age. See more detail in "The Spirit and the Word," 199-227.

[463] Prophets' (particularly Jeremiah) reserve about the Spirit may have been due to conflicts with prophets who claimed and boasted their possession of the *ruah* of God. See Edmond Jacob, *Theology of the Old Testament*, translated by Arthur. W. Heathcote and Philip J. Allcock (London: Hodder & Stoughton 1958), 125.

Jeremiah also has to tackle the prophetic claims of his contemporaries and as a consequence spirit for him is only wind.

5.6. The Spirit of God and the Word of God in Jeremiah: Implicit use of the Spirit of God in the Book of Jeremiah

Before going to the study on the use of "the word of God" in Jeremiah, one has to note that the pre-exilic canonical prophets appealed to "the word" rather than to "the spirit" of Yahweh in order to validate their pronouncements.[464] Therefore, as discussed in the forgoing study, the exact word Spirit of God is avoided in Jeremiah. However, spirit is used in connection with God in many instances. Therefore, one is tempted to investigate the reason behind the implicit use of Spirit of God in Jeremiah.

One reason may probably be suggested by the popular use of "word of God" in prophetic literatures.[465] Word in many cases overlaps with that of the spirit, and indeed Jewish thought was never able to make a precise delimitation between them.[466] Thus, for the prophets, the "word" takes the place for "spirit" which in the popular thinking is the cosmic power of God.[467] However, they are also used side by side as synonymous.[468] Kaufmann maintains that the essential characteristic of Israelite prophecy in the proclamation of the word of Yahweh. The effect of the Spirit of Yahweh on people is regarded in the Old Testament, not as the cause of prophecy but, at the very most, as a by – product of prophetical experience.[469] The

---

[464] Keith W. Carley, *Ezekiel among the Prophets* (London: SCM Press Ltd., 1975), 56.

[465] In a similar fashion with that of ANE religious beliefs, the "word of God" has been considered the potent medium of divine power which effectively influences events. Side by side with the divine word in the law, with its validity for all occasion we find the particular proclamation of the divine will for particular situations, that is the prophetic word of God See Walter Eichrodt, *Theology of the Old Testament,* Vol. 2, translated by J.A. Baker (London: SCM Press Ltd., 1967), 72.

[466] Eichrodt, *Theology of the Old Testament* Vol. 2, 79.

[467] Cf. Jer. 1:5, 9; Ezek. 2:4ff; 3:1; Isa. 55:10f.

[468] See parallel usage in II Sam. 23:2; Ps. 33:6; Isa. 59:21.

[469] Cited by Menahem Haran, in "From Early to Classical Prophecy: Continuity and Change," *Vetus Testamentum* XXVII/4 (October, 1977): 396.

idea of embodied word becomes particularly apparent in Jeremiah and Ezekiel. In Jeremiah 1:9 (Cf. Ezek. 3:1-2), the word of God is placed by the hand directly into Jeremiah's mouth; the word is conveyed into his very being without having been spoken. The word of God is enfleshed in the very person of the prophet and it is not only what the prophet speaks but also who he is that now constitutes the word of God.[470] Thus, the "word of God" is not a disembodied word; it is a personal word spoken in personal encounter.

Schweitzer asserts that while spirit is a stronger expression for the overwhelming, often incomprehensible power of the divine event, "word" underscores the other side of it. That is why Jeremiah can say that the false prophets will become wind and the "word" is not in them (Cf. 5:13).[471] The spirit reaches its goal only when it becomes identical with the word (Cf. Job. 26:14; Ps. 139:14). The divine word is central to Jeremiah's preaching; in fact it is his preaching.[472] Honeycutt expresses that the person (or persons) responsible for the canonical form of the book of Jeremiah was governed by the dominance of "the Word of ... from the Lord" as a cohesive power of the book.[473] It is creative, constructive and self-fulfilling (1:12; 4:28; 20:8-9; 23:29). A hint of hypostatisation of the word (*dabar*) is traced in the book of Jeremiah.[474] Mowinckel asserts that the reforming prophets emphatically stress the fact that they have received Yahweh's word; they do not derive their power from or authenticate their prophetic call by the conception of Yahweh's spirit,

---

[470] Terence E. Fretheim, "Word of God" *ABD* Vol. 6, edited by David Noel Freedman et. al., (New York: Doubleday, 1992), 966.

[471] Albert Schweitzer, *The Holy Spirit*, translated by Reginald H. and Ilse Fuller (Philadelphia: Fortress Press, 1978), 22.

[472] Jack R. Lundbom, "Book of Jeremiah," *ABD* Vol. 3, 719. The noun form of דבר is found 1440 times in the Old Testament in which it occurs 204 times in the book of Jeremiah, the most frequent occurrences in the entire books of the Old Testament. See G. Gerleman, "דבר, " in *TLOT* Vol. I, 325-332.

[473] Roy L. Honeycutt, "Jeremiah The Prophet and the Book" *Review and Expositor* LXXVIII/3 (Sum. 1981): 307.

[474] See detailed discussion in W.H. Schmidt, "דבר" in *TDOT* Vol. 3, edited by G. Johannes Botterweck et. al., translated by John T. Willis (Grand Rapids, Michigan: Eerdmans Pub. Co., 1978), 120-121.

which, in fact, they have rejected, but by their own consciousness of possessing his word.[475] This is clearly shown in Jeremiah who chooses the word *ruah* to express his scornful allusion to the spirit possession of the nebhi'ism (5:13).[476] For Jeremiah, those ecstatic individuals, who have not got "the word" in them, will turn לרוח, that is "wind-men" or "nothing-men." Therefore, we may conclude that Jeremiah's implicit use of the Spirit of God and his preference to the word is resulted by two current issues: 1) the continuing emphasis on the centrality of the word of God as a disembodied word; 2) prophetic opposition to the false prophets who claimed to have possessed the Spirit of God to authenticate their oracles.

5.7. Parallel References to the Spirit of God in the Book of Jeremiah

As stated in the forgoing study, the prophet's attitude to the contemporary prophets led him to avoid the use of the phrase the Spirit of God. If the literature is studied along with other exilic prophetic literature, we can find parallel and equivalent expressions in different parts of the texts in relation to the Spirit of God. Apart from direct reference to spirit in relation to God, there are significant terms, which are more or less related expressions synonymous to the Spirit of God, found in the prophecy. One of these is found with the promise of a new covenant in Jeremiah 31:31-34. Therefore, exegetical study of the text will illustrate the meaning and significance of the Spirit of God in the book of Jeremiah.

---

[475] Mowinckel, "The Spirit and the Word," 225.

[476] The reforming prophets' (including Jeremiah's) disapproval or reservation to use the *ruah* of God may probably be caused by the association of the *ruah* idea with extreme manifestations of nebhi'ism, and on the other hand that this ecstatic element in its primitive and exaggerated forms is very much toned down in the reforming prophets, whose own spiritual temper and attitude would, if anything, cause them to see such excesses in an unsympathetic light. See Mowinckel, "The Spirit and the Word," 207.

5.8. The Spirit of God and the New Covenant: Exegetical Study of Jer. 31:31-34

Why do we deal with Jeremiah 31:31-34 in relation to the study of Spirit of God, which in fact does not mention the word "Spirit of God" or even "spirit" in the passage? This would be answered by quoting Clements who says, "Although the word Spirit (*ruah*) is not used (in this passage), the implication is certainly that God's spirit will move the hearts of Israel to be obedient to the divine law."[477] Davidson also writes, "Jeremiah does not use the expression (putting the Spirit of God in human's hearts), though his promise that Jehovah (sic) will write his law on men's (sic) hearts seems to have much the same sense, or at lest it expresses the new Spirit of Ezekiel."[478] Therefore, the passage shares similar thought in relation to the understanding of the Spirit of God with that of other exilic prophets.[479] With the help of form-critical and textual analysis of our selected passage, we will try to delineate the meaning and significance of the Spirit of God in the book of Jeremiah.

5.8.1. Text: Jeremiah 31:31-34

v. 31: [a]*Behold the days are coming,*[a] *says the Lord; I shall make a new covenant with the house of Israel and with the* [b]*house of Judah.*[b]

v. 32: *It will not be like a covenant that I made with their fathers in the day I took them by the hand to bring them out of the land of Egypt* [a]*a covenant which they broke,*[a] *though I was their husband,*[b] *says the Lord.*

v. 33: *But this is the covenant which I shall make with the house of Israel*[a] *after those days says the Lord: I shall put*[b] *my law in their*

[477] R.E. Clements, *Jeremiah Interpretation*, edited by J.L. Mayes et al., (Atlanta: John Knox Press, 1988), 190.

[478] A.B. Davidson, *The Book of the Prophet Ezekiel* (Cambridge: Cambridge Univ. Press, 1892), 264.

[479] According to Patrick D. Miller, the languages and images or newness are important in the restoration promises of other prophets as well, including a new heart, a new spirit and a new thing. The similarity of this text to Ezekiel's prophecy is that it will be brought to happen by divine action. See "The Book of Jeremiah" *NIB* Vol. VI, edited by Leander E. Keck et al., (Nashville: Abingdon Press, 2001), 812.

midst and I shall write it on their hearts; and I will be their God and they shall be my people.

v. 34: *No longer shall a man teach his friend nor a man will say to his brother "Know Yahweh,[a]" for they shall all know me, from the least to the greatest, says the Lord; for I will forgive their iniquity and remember their sin no more.*

5.8.2. Text Critical Notes

v. 31 [a-a] *Behold the days are coming* is an announcement of restoration (of hope). This oracular formula is called an "eschatological phrase" as it calls for future events.[480]

v. 31 [b-b] Rudolph deletes it because it is lacking in v. 33; he understands "house of Israel" to refer to the northern kingdom and not the whole people of north and south.[481] Holladay retains it as the clause finds parallel with 11:10b.[482] Many commentators think that this should be deleted since "the house of Israel" seems in this passage refers to the whole people.[483] Thus, "the house of Judah" may be deleted.

v. 32 [a-a] *a covenant which they broke* is the unusual syntax, in which the half verse begins with a conjunction. Here the repetition of אשר implies the repetition of the main idea.[484] The verb הפר hiphil perfect form of פרר may refer to breaking the covenant by the exodus ancestors, by Jeremiah's audience, and by all the generations in between.

---

480 H. Cunliff Jones, *Jeremiah: God in History* (London: SCM Press Ltd., 1966 (revised edn.), 197.

481 Cited by Carroll, *Jeremiah: A Commentary,* 610.

482 William L. Holladay, *Jeremiah II* (Philadelphia: Fortress Press, 1986), 197.

483 See John Bright, *Jeremiah: The Anchor Bible,* 203; also L. Elliot Binns, *The Book of the Prophet Jeremiah* (London: SCM Press Ltd., 1919), 203.

484 The suppression of the retrospective pronoun takes the place especially when it would represent an accusative of the object, or when it would be a separate pronoun representing a nominative of the subject in a noun clause. Instead of a retrospective pronoun the main idea itself is repeated, most probably due to subsequent amplification of the original text by another hand. See A.E. Cowley (ed), *Gesenius' Hebrew Grammar*, revised by E. Kautsch (2nd Eng. Ed.), (Oxford: Clarendon Press, 1910), 445.

v. 32 [b-b] *I was their husband*: The MT is corrected by the Greek (LXX) "…and I disregarded them" and Syriac has, " I abhorred/loathed" Carroll suggests to maintain בעל – "to abhor" which makes a better divine response to the broken covenant.[485] The MT reading "husband" could also be represented "Lord or "master" as בעל could also be translated as "lord" "Baal."[486] The verb בעל (lit. to marry) is an emphasis in the rights and authority the husband exercised over his wife or concubine.[487] It is to be retained, as Yahweh is understood as the superior partner in the covenant, while Israel is the inferior partner.

v. 33 [a] *House of Israel*: The promise unites the two houses of v. 31 into the one "house of Israel." Some manuscripts render it "children of Israel" (בני). It is agreeable when Keown and others comment that "children" makes sense and more explicit by adopting the old Pentateuchal term for the covenant people as a whole (Cf. Ex. 19:3-6).[488] Clements prefers "בית" (house) instead of children as a significant title for the people scattered in diaspora.[489] Since "house" is a synonym for "people" in many instances it needs no emendation.

v. 33 [b] Literally "I shall give." Several manuscripts add waw consecutive (w) to MT's perfect of נתן thus render "Then I shall put." However some hold a view that the perfect could stand alone in its prophetic sense.[490] The meaning of the text almost remains the same.

v. 34 [a] Here in verse 34 a salvation oracle in the form of a change of speech from first person to the third person is applied. The expression "know Yahweh" is not a form of command or request found elsewhere in the Old Testament.[491] Therefore, it is a characteristic use of Jeremiah.

---

[485] Carroll, *Jeremiah: A Commentary*, 132.

[486] See Brown Driver Briggs, *Lexicon*, 127.

[487] G.L. Keown, P.J. Scalise and T.G. Smothers, Jeremiah *26-52: Word Biblical Commentary*, (Dallas, Texas: Word Books, Publisher, 1998), 132. (Cf. Gen. 21:13; 22:22; 24:1; Hos. 2:16).

[488] G.L. Keown, P.J. Scalise and T.G. Smothers, *Jeremiah 26-52 WBC*, 132.

[489] R.E. Clements, *Jeremiah: Interpretation*, 191.

[490] G.L. Keown, P.J. Scalise, and T.G. Smothers, *Jeremiah 26-52: WBC*, 134.

[491] The closest expression is found in Prov. 3:6, which speaks: "In all your ways know him."

5.8.3. Form Critical Notes

The promise of New Covenant (31:31-34) is one of the most famous passages in the book as it is the only reference to a new covenant in the Old Testament.[492] This section known as "the promise of a new covenant" is found in what is called "the book of consolation" (Jer. 30-33).[493] According to Clements, chapters 30-33 could be taken together as a unit which speaks of the promise of restoration. This unit thus consistently and glowingly exposes a message of hope of an eventual restoration of Israel to its land.[494] The so-called book of consolation consists of (1) Promise of restoration (30:1-24) (2) Promise of return of the exiles and the new covenant (31:1-40), Jeremiah's purchase of a field of Anathoth (32:1-44), and Promise of restoration (33:1-26). The Book of Consolation in this chapter (31) consists of five short salvation oracles which form a chiasm centered on the promise of the new covenant (31-34).[495]

The new covenant (31:31-34) begins with the eschatological formula, "the days are coming." In this proclamation of salvation, the Lord, speaking in the first person, promises to make a new covenant with Israel and Judah to forgive their sin. A change in speech pattern is found in v.34 from first to the third person, presented as the consequence of the fulfillment of this promise. The passage (31:31-34) is structurally divided into two, (a) a prose section (vv. 31-33. a) and (b) a poetic section (vv. 33b-34). This is also marked by chiastic

---

[492] But the language and images of such newness are important in the restoration promises of other prophets, including a new heart, a new spirit (Ezek. 11:19-20; 18:31; 36:26) and new things (Isa. 42:9; 43:19; 48:6).

[493] Technically the book of consolation consists of chapters 30-31 only because the narratives in chs. 32-33 are redaction of the second part of Jeremiah's tradition which deal with positive future of the community. See Robert P. Carroll, *From Chaos to Covenant*, 204.

[494] R.E. Clements, *Jeremiah: Interpretation*, edited by James Luther Mays et. al., (Atlanta: John Knox Press, 1988), 175.

[495] The first (vv 23–26) and fifth (vv 38–40) oracles are about Jerusalem. The second (vv 27–30) and fourth (vv 35–37) form a contrasting pair. See G.L. Keown, P.J. Scalise, and T.G. Smothers, *Jeremiah 26-52: WBC*, 127.

forms- the first centering on the old covenant and the second on the law.[496]

The first section, though in prose has a careful structure, beginning with the word "days" (in vv. 31, 33), continuing inward with the word "I will make a new covenant with the house of Israel (vv. 31, 33). This statement is added further by references to the old covenant (v.32). Thus forming the centre of the prose section in verse 32.[497] The poetic section (33b-34) begins with two first-person singular verbs, "I will put my law in their midst and I shall write it on their hearts;" and closed with promise of forgiveness. According to Huey, a new covenant revealed to Jeremiah in this passage is not another covenant renewal but an internal transformation of the people based upon the divine provision of complete forgiveness.[498] It has a close connection with the Deuteronomistic redaction of the tradition (Cf. 11:1-11; 34:8-22).[499] The covenant formula is used elsewhere in the book of Jeremiah.[500] The theme of the new covenant "putting the law of God in the midst and writing in the hearts of the people" is also well known in other prophecies especially in Ezekiel 11:20; 36:28 where the Spirit of God plays significant role.

With regard to the setting there has been variety of views. Considerable numbers of scholars consider the book of consolation and the prophecy of new covenant (31: 31-34) to be the authentic words of Jeremiah. John Bright writes, "...the authenticity ought never to have been questioned."[501] However, doubt about the

---

[496] Cf. Holladay, *Jeremiah* II, 197.

[497] See William L. Holladay, *Jeremiah a Fresh Reading* (New York: The Pilgrim Press, 1990), 129f.

[498] Huey Jr., *Jeremiah and Lamentation*, 281. But von Rad argues that this new covenant is to be understood as a radically new type of covenant. See *Old Testament Theology II*, (New York: Harper & Row, 1965), 212.

[499] According to Carroll the prose oracles of tradition including Jer. 31:31 suggests a Deuteronomistic redaction and poetic oracles of Jeremiah do not contain any reference to the covenant. See more detail in Carroll, *From Chaos to Covenant*, 217f.

[500] The formula "I will be their God and they will be my people," is also found in Jer. 7:23; 24:7; 30:22; 31:1; 32:38.

[501] John Bright, *Jeremiah Anchor Bible*, 287.

authenticity of the oracle is not silent concerning the authorship of the prophecy.[502] Some reject the authenticity claiming that it was either an exilic or a post-exilic reflection, as shown by the Deuteronomic shaping of language and thought in the passage.[503] There are more scholars who opt for a middle part, i.e., a reworking of the prophet's *ipissima verba* by a later redactor.[504]

One group of school that accepts the authenticity of the passage claims that it was originating during the reign of Josiah, in the silent period of Jeremiah's ministry.[505] Holladay suggests that Jer. 31:31-34 is occasioned by the recitation of Deuteronomy at a festival of booths in 587 BCE.[506] Looking at the ethological contents, one could have observed proximity with the prophecy of restoration found elsewhere in the book. Thus we may conclude that the passage contains the genuine sayings of Jeremiah, addressed to northern Israel and uttered relatively early in is career. The oracle passed through the hands of an editor or editors who may have been responsible for some expansion or adaptation of Jeremiah's thought to a later situation.

---

[502] Those who accept the authenticity of the prophecy include such as Cornill, W.J. Moulton, L. Elliot Binns, etc., See L. Elliot Binns, *The Book of the Prophet Jeremiah*, 241, 244.

[503] Those who reject are such as Smend, Stade, Duhm, Movers, De Wette, Hitzig, etc. See Binns, *The Book of the Prophet Jeremiah*, 241, and George Adam Smith, *Jeremiah* (London: Hodder and Stoughton, 1929), 375.

[504] This is advocated by many of modern commentators. For Example, R. E. Clements, H. Cunliff Jones, Bohmer, Herrmann, Nicholson, Thiel, Carroll, and others. See Carroll, *Jeremiah*, 613., Jones, *Jeremiah*: *God in History*, 197., R.E. Clements, *Jeremiah Interpretation*, 176.

[505] This school maintains that the so-called "new covenant" reflects the Josianic reform in 621. It was the outcome of Jeremiah's silent and private meditation in the period between the beginning of the Deuteronomic reform and the death of Josiah (6212-609). See Elmer E. Leslie, *Jeremiah Chronologically Arranged, Translated and Interpreted* (New York: Abingdon Press, nd.), 336.

[506] According to biblical records, during the time, Johannan and his forces caught up Ishmael with them and freed the civilians who were caught by Ishmael (Jer. 42:2). Among them was Jeremiah. Following the events Johannan gathered his group to move south, in tending to go to Egypt. In their way to south they might have stopped in Jerusalem and observed a festival of booth where recitation of Deuteronomy was heard (in 587) (Cf. Jer. 41:17-18). Thus this was the occasion for Jeremiah's proclamation of the new covenant. See Holladay, *Jeremiah I*, 35.

5.8.4. Comments in Relation to the Meaning and Significance of the Spirit of God

The foregoing study of the passage reveals that the promise of a new covenant is a proclamation occasioned by the deep darkness of exilic experience.[507] It is a promise of restoration for the whole people, both Judah and Israel. The promise described in v. 31 is significant because it is a "new" covenant. The word "new" according to Holladay figures largely in the hopeful words of the prophets of exile.[508] Newness as the effect of the Spirit of God is emphasized here in v.31 as "making a new ברית.[509] In the following verse, the statement of v. 31 is negated by saying that the old covenant is failed because it has been broken by the exodus ancestors, by Jeremiah's audience, and by all the generations in between.[510] Vv. 33 and 34 describe the unique differences of the new covenant. H. Wolf acknowledges that the first completely new element in the new covenant is the manner in which God's guiding directions would be mediated.[511] This new elements in the "after days" are "setting his law (תורה) within them (בקרבם) and writing (כתב) in their hearts (לבב). Thus the phrase "after those days" synthesizes two motifs: the coming days of restoration after which a new covenant will be enacted; it being a further event in the programme of restoration.[512] "Putting the law of God within them" and "writing in their hearts," a nature of radical change in inner being is also emphasized elsewhere in the other exilic prophets.

Thus the change is emphasized by reference of a new heart and a new spirit (Ezek. 18:31; 36:26). It is also to be performed by God's *spirit* (Ezek. 36:27; 37:14). The old covenant is dead; instead there

---

[507] Supposing the passage coming by the time following the fall of Jerusalem in 587 BCE.

[508] Cf. new heart/new spirit in Ezek. 18:31; 11:19; 36:26; and new things in Isaiah 42:8. See more detail in Holladay, *Jeremiah* I, 197.

[509] The verse renders that when the new *berith* is instituted the house of Israel will become Yahweh's people. See Carroll, *Jeremiah, A Commentary*, 610f.

[510] G.L. Keown, P.J. Scalise, and T.G. Smothers, *Jeremiah 26-52: WBC*, 131.

[511] H. W. Wolf, *Confrontations with Prophets* (Philadelphia: Fortress Press, 1983), 54.

[512] Carroll, *Jeremiah, A Commentary*, 610.

will be an inner power and motivation towards obedience on the part of Israel, written on the very hearts of the people. This is what the contemporary prophet Ezekiel assigns to be achieved by the Spirit of God.[513] Thus the effect of the Spirit of God leads to a universal knowledge of God which will be given through the operation of the Spirit of God (Cf. Ezek. 39:27ff.).

The meaning of the new covenant may possibly be understood in the light of the so-called *Bundesformel* (covenant formula) of the exilic prophets.[514] According to Raitt prophets of the exile, such as Jeremiah and Ezekiel proclaim and foresee the genuine relationship between God and Israel which is represented in the *bundesformel.*[515] Some scholars are in the opinion that both Jeremiah and Ezekiel affirm the relationship between God and the people in which deliverance and eschatological dimension are to be found.[516] Fohrer who studied the oracles of deliverance acknowledges that the *bundesformel* seen in Ezekiel has a repeatedly employed term; that is "You are my people; I am your God."[517] The occurrence of the *bundesformel*, however, is characterized by the active involvement of the Spirit of God.[518] Raitt argues that Ezekiel's *bundesformel* is parallel to the speech of Jeremiah of the new covenant (31:31-34) and points to the closest and most far-reaching relationship between God and man (sic). It enhances the communion between God and the man (sic) newly created in his inner life (by divine spirit) as the inner

---

[513] In spite of similar theological understanding, Jeremiah is distinct from other exilic prophets who acknowledge the operation of the *ruah* of God in the life and activities of the exilic community. Jeremiah, though sharing the same understanding of the *ruah* of God avoids using it for his conflict with his contemporary prophets.

[514] The term 'Bundesformel" is coined by Rudolph Smend to refer to the covenant formula which is represented in the statement: "I will be your God and you will be my people."

[515] Raitt, *A Theology of Exile*, 198. Cf. Jer. 24:7; 31:33; 32:38; Ezek. 11:20; 34:30; 36:28; 37:2, 27.

[516] Thus Arthur Weiser, Rudolph and George Fohrer have this opinion. See Raitt, *A Theology of Exile*, 178ff.

[517] Cited by Raitt in *A Theology of Exile*, 198.

[518] See Ezek. 11:19; 36:26; 37:14; 39:29.

goal and result of redemption.[519] In line with Raitt, both Eichrodt and von Rad feel that the notion of a new covenant in Jeremiah is present by implication in Ezekiel's great promise of restoration.[520] Raitt argues that those two oracles in Ezekiel - 34:25-31 & 37:24-28 (cf. 36:26; 37:14) stand in integrity with Jeremiah 31:31-34 & 32:36-41. The source and pattern of Ezekiel's hope for deliverance are the source of Jeremiah's.[521] Therefore, we may conclude that the new covenant in the book of Jeremiah is parallel to newness of life or transformed life in the book of Ezekiel, which is attained, with the empowering endowment of the Spirit of God. Thus the Spirit of God is the transforming power of God which brought radical change of inner life.

5.9. Summary

The above discussion shows that prophet Jeremiah who first experienced the tragedy of destruction and exile exercised his ministry in the contemporary situations, proclaiming both judgment and hope of restoration to the suffering community. Though redactional activity of the literature is well represented, the authenticity of the central core is widely accepted. As one of the exilic prophets his prophecy shares both distinction and similarity with that of other exilic prophets. The understanding of the Spirit of God is significant in Jeremiah, in which spirit is frequently used in connection with God; which, however, is not attributed as the Spirit of God. The distinctive characteristic of the prophecy is acknowledged in the understanding of *ruah* and the Spirit of God. The prophet's hesitation to use the term Spirit of God is clearly manifested. This is possibly because of his conflict with the contemporary prophets who claimed the inspiration of the Spirit of God, which, for him is only "wind." For the prophet, spirit is wind/air, breath or spirit, which is distinct from the personality of God. It is rather the "word" of God,

---

[519] Raitt, *A Theology of Exile*, 198.

[520] See von Rad, *Theology of the Old Testament* Vol. II (New York: Harper & Row, 1965), 235. Also Water Eichrodt, *Ezekiel, A Commentary*, translated by Cosslett Quin (London: SCM Press Ltd., 1970), 501-502.

[521] Thus parallel use in the two prophets. See Raitt, *A Theology of Exile*, 206.

which represents the power of God in his activity. However, his use of the term *ruah* (spirit) in the book of Jeremiah attests that *ruah* is the life-giving power, both creative and destructive in its operation, manifested in various forms. Thus, *ruah* is under the direction and control of God and therefore it is safe to call it the Spirit of God. Therefore, for the prophet, the Spirit of God signifies God's agent of life-giving activity and destroying power.

An exegetical study of the selected passage (31:31-34) shows that the oracle of the new covenant is one of the restoration promises shared by the exilic prophets. Even though the term Spirit of God is not employed, the new covenant with putting and writing the law of God in the hearts of the people signifies a new empowerment of the exiles. Thus, it is parallel with a "new heart" and a "new spirit" of Ezekiel and a "new thing" of Deutero-Isaiah. The promise of new covenant to the exiles indicates giving of new life with new heart and new spirit. This is to be achieved by the transforming power of the Spirit of God. Thus, the Spirit of God for Jeremiah is an enabling agent of God to achieve his will, and a dynamic force sent by God operating in the restoration and transformation of his people.

Conclusion

1. Concluding Remarks

From the foregoing study of the meaning and significance of the Spirit of God, the following conclusions can be drawn:

1) The term רוח (spirit) primarily signifies a movement of air in the form of breath or wind, which however could also be a "spirit" in an anthropological and religious sphere. Whether used as a literal/ profane as wind/breath of God or as anthropological and theological term as Spirit of God, the distinctive and dynamic power of God is emphasized. Various representations of the term in relation to God as Spirit Elohim, *spirit Adonai* or Spirit Elohim or with suffixes have different meaning and significance depending on the contexts.

2) Along with the development of religious understanding in Israel, the Old Testament concept of the Spirit of God had also been developed in course of time. The Spirit of God is an empowering dynamic force which is associated with ecstatic prophecy in the earliest period. It became an equipment to become a king. For the pre-exilic classical prophets it signifies the divine quality with ethical dimension. The Spirit of God for Wisdom and Poetry is the life-giving and creative power of the divine, which is a source of all life and wisdom. One has to observe that the development of the concept in the Old Testament period had been caused by the socio-political and religious contexts, known as the historical situations of the time.

3) Exilic communities of both the exiles in Babylonia and in the homeland lost their socio-economic and political status and suffered a kind of rejection and oppression from powerful nations. Various responses to the exilic tragedy could be observed in the literature of the exilic age. As historical situations had shaped various theological understanding of the Old Testament, the exilic age was also marked by the development of profound theological ideas including the understanding of the Spirit of God.

4) In the painful experiences of deportation and the exile, prophets of the same age brought out distinctive religious teachings with a distinctive theological understanding of the Spirit of God. The Spirit of God became a significant dynamic power with a new meaning for the exilic community that were under painful situations. With the growing tradition of prophetic literature, the Spirit of God has become a distinctive theological thought with specific meanings and significations in the reshaping of Israel's religious tradition.

5) The book of Ezekiel represents a description of the Spirit of God in many instances. The Spirit of God for Ezekiel is the divine power operating in various ways. The Spirit of God is a moving force, which is responsible for displacement of the prophet in his visionary experiences. It is not only a moving force; it is an inspiring force that prepared the prophet for prophecy. It is significant to note that the Spirit of God for Ezekiel is the divine power that transforms the exilic community so that God would deliver them from their captivity. As demonstrated in the vision of dry bones, it is reassuring for the exilic community that the Spirit of God plays a role of restoring people from the countries of their enemies as the Spirit of God gives life to the lifeless bones.

6) The prophetic eschatological promise of Ezekiel is significant that the permanent endowment of the Spirit of God to the house of Israel is explicitly demonstrated. This promise is described as God's renewal and fulfilment of the covenant. "Pouring the Spirit of God upon the house of Israel" signifies that God would never leave his people any more. Thus, the Spirit of God gives hope of continued blessing and permanent presence of God with the exilic community.

7) The book of Deutero-Isaiah portrays the Spirit of God with an ethical significance. For Deutero-Isaiah, the Spirit of God is the

divine power endowed upon Cyrus, the appointed servant of the Lord. It plays a role of establishing *mishpat* not only for the Israelites, but also for the whole earth. The exilic community is reassured that the coming king would be one upon whom God endows his *spirit* for them so that *mishpat* will be established on earth. The universal role of the Spirit of God is a significant theme for Deutero-Isaiah. When he speaks about pouring the Spirit of God upon the descendants of Israel, he also conceded that gentiles would also benefit it. The Spirit of God is the divine power operating in the salvation of human kind, both now and in the future, not only for Israelites, but also for the Gentiles.

8) Like prophet Ezekiel, Deutero-Isaiah also claims that the Spirit of God is upon him that his proclamation is authentic. In the context of doubts about the divine plan of salvation among the exilic community, the prophet claims that God sends him and God's spirit is also endowed upon him so that his proclamation is just and truthful. Therefore, the Spirit of God is the divine empowering power, the authenticated word of God for prophetic proclamation.

9) The understanding of the Spirit of God is significant in Jeremiah wherein *ruah* is frequently used in connection with God; which, however, is not attributed as the Spirit of God. The prophet's hesitation to use the term "Spirit of God" is possibly caused by his conflict with the contemporary prophets who claimed the inspiration of the Spirit of God. For him it is rather the "word" of God, which represents the power of God in his activity. However, the use of the term "*ruah*" in the book of Jeremiah attests that spirit is the life-giving power of God, both creative and destructive in its operation, manifested in various forms.

10) While the term "the Spirit of God" is not employed in the new covenant oracle (31:31-34) of Jeremiah, it is clear that the passage is one of the restoration promises shared by the exilic prophets. The new covenant with putting and writing the law of God in the hearts of the people signifies a new empowerment of the exiles. In parallel with other exilic prophets, Jeremiah acknowledges that the promise of restoration is to be achieved by the transforming power of the Spirit of God.

11. From the exegetical studies we can conclude that in the writings of the exilic prophets, the Spirit of God is not portrayed as a distinct personality from God. It is the empowering and restoring power of God operated in the lives of the exilic community. According to the exilic prophets, the Spirit of God inspired prophetic proclamation, strengthened the leaders, empowered the people. It is an enabling dynamic power of God, which prepared the exilic community to be a transformed, living, and restored community in the exilic age.

2. Implications of the Study for Formulation of Contextual Pneumatology

From the foregoing study we can conclude that the Spirit of God, in the Old Testament is seen as a dynamic force operating variedly with the changing contexts. It is in the exilic age, that the Spirit of God inspires the prophets for their proclamation. It is a promised dynamic power of God, who establishes justice on the whole earth and restores the exilic community to their own land. It plays a role of creating a just society by inspiring an eschatological vision of the prophets of the time. Prophets of the exilic age formulated the doctrine of the Spirit of God which meets the needs of the community. Therefore, one could have assumed that the concept of the Spirit of God is a developing concept that equipped the community to respond to the theological crises of the time. In short, it is the dynamic power that functions in the socio-political and religious contexts of the exilic community.

How far the concept of the Spirit of God in the Old Testament can be applied in the contemporary church where the person and work of the Spirit of God is portrayed in diverse ways? What will be the implications of the meaning and significance of the Spirit of God within the exilic period for contemporary deliberations on the Spirit of God?

From the preceding study it has been made clear that the Spirit of God is the dynamic power, operating in the socio-political and religious contexts of the community. It challenges the doubts of the community by inspiring and equipping the prophets to proclaim the divine plan of salvation. The Spirit of God inspires prophetic proclamation in the context of apostasy, doubts, and fears. Permanent bestowal of the Spirit of God is promised upon the descendants. In the context of plurality of ideologies and beliefs, the church is therefore, persuaded that she is inspired and permanently equipped with the Spirit of God in her proclamation.

In the context of oppression and subjugation, the Spirit of God prepares the servant king to establish *mishpat.* The comforting promise of transformation and restoration found in the book of Jeremiah and Ezekiel give new hope and new life for the lifeless exiles. The eschatological hope that is to be realized with the pouring of the Spirit of God gives a hope for the oppressed and the suffering community. Thus, the Spirit of God plays a liberative role by providing a hope for the hopeless in the context of oppressions.

The universal aspect of the role of the Spirit of God is clearly portrayed in the writings of the exilic prophets. For Isaiah, the Spirit of God will empower the elected king to establish *mishpat* not only for Israelites, but also for the whole earth. The universal role of the Spirit of God is a foretaste for dialogue and mission of the church to the whole nations. The portrayal of the Spirit of God in the writings of the exilic prophets typifies the formulation of biblical theology in contexts. It demonstrates the presentation of the meaning and function of the Spirit of God in today's context. The formulation of today's pneumatology should therefore address the socio-political and religious needs of humankind.

Bibliography

A. Primary Source

Charles Thompson (trans). *The Septuagint Bible*, edited, revised and enlarged by G.A. Muses. Colorado: Indian Hills, 1954.

Ellinger K. E. and Rudolph W. (eds), *Biblia Hebraica Stuttgartensia*. Stuttgart: Deutsche Bibelgeselschafgt, 1967/1977.

The Holy Bible: The New Revised Standard Version. Nashville, Tennessee: Catholic Bible Press, 1993.

B. Secondary Source

I. Bibles & Translations

Kittel, Rudolph (ed). *Biblia Hebraica*. Stuttgart: Wurttembergische Bibelanstaltt Stuttgart, 1937. (3rd edn.).

Muses, G.A. (ed), *The Septuagint Bible*, translated by Charles Thompson. Colorado: Indian Hills, 1954.

The Holy Bible: New English Bible with the Apocrypha. Great Britain: The Oxford University Press, 1970.

The Holy Bible: Revised Standard Version. Grand Rapids: Zondervan Publishers, 1971.

The Holy Bible: New International Version. New York: International Bible Society, 1978.

The Holy Bible: New Jerusalem Bible. London: Darton, Longman & Todd Ltd., 1985.

The Holy Bible: Authorized King James Version. Nashville: Thomas Nelson Inc., Publishers, 1995.

II. Lexicons, Dictionaries, Encyclopaedia

Albertz, Rainer and Westermann, Claus. "רוח" *TLOT* Vol-3, edited by Ernst Jenni & Claus Westermann, translated by Mark E. Biddle. Massachusetts: Hendrickson Publishers, 1977. 1202-1220.

Arndt, F. and Gingrich, F. Wilbur. *A Greek English Lexicon of the New Testament and Other Early Christian Literature.* Chicago: The University of Chicago Press, 1979.

Baumgartel, Fredrich. Spirit in the OT," *TDNT* Vol. 6., edited by Gerhard Friedrich, trans. & ed. in English by G.W. Bromiley. Grand Rapids, Michigan: WMB Eerdmans, 1968. 359-368.

Brown, Francis, Driver, S.R. & Briggs, Charles A. *A Hebrew and English Lexicon of the Old Testament.* Oxford: Clarendon Press, 1968.

Davidson, Benjamin. *The Analytical Hebrew and Chaldee Lexicon.* Lynn: Masachusets: Hendrickson Publishers, Inc., 1981.

Fredericks, D.C. "נשמה" *NIDOTTE* Vol. 3, edited by William A. van Gemeren et.al. UK: Paternoster Press, 1996. 1070-1078.

Fretheim, Terence E. "Word of God" *ABD* Vol. 6, edited by David Noel Freedman et. al. New York : Doubleday, 1992.

Gerleman, G. "דבר" in *TLOT* Vol. I, edited by Ernst Jenni & Claus Westermann, translated by Mark E. Biddle. Massachusetts: Hendrickson Publishers, 1977. 325-332.

Horn, F.W. "Holy Spirit" *ABD* Vol. 3, translated by Dietlinde E. Elliot, edited by Noel Freedman et al. New York: Doubleday, 1992.

Hoyle, R. Birch. "Spirit (Holy Spirit), Spirit of God" *Encyclopedia of Religion and Ethics Vol. XI*, edited by James Hastings et. al., New York: Charles Scribner's Sons. 1920. 784-803.

Kohler, Ludwig and Baumgartner, Walter. "רוח" Hebrew *and Aramaic Lexicon of the Old Testament* Vol. 2. Translated and Edited by M. E. J. Richardson. Leiden: Brill, 2000. 1195-1201.

Lundbom, Jack R. "Book of Jeremiah" *ABD* Vol. 3, edited by Noel Freedman et al. New York: Doubleday, 1992.

Pfeiffer, C.F. "History of the People of Israel," *ISBE* Vol. 2, Edited by Geoffrey W Bromiley et. al. Grand Rapids, Michigan: Eerdmans, 1988.

Sack, Ronal H. "Nabonidus" *Anchor Bible Dictionary* Vol. 4, edited by Noel Freedman et al. New York: Doubleday, 1992.

Schmidt, W.H. "דבר" in *TDOT* Vol. 3, edited by G. Johannes Botterweck et. al., translated by John T. Willis. Grand Rapids, Michigan: Eerdmans, 1978. 84-125.

Seebas. "נפש" *TDOT* Vol. IX, edited by G. Johannes Botterweck et. al., translated by David Green. Grand Rapids, Michigan: Eerdmans, 1998. 497-519.

Soderlund, S.K. "Book of Jeremiah" *ISBE* Vol. 2 (E-Z), edited by Geoffrey W. Bromiley et. al. Grand Rapids, Michigan: Eerdmans, 1988.

Turner, M. "Spiritual Gifts" *New Dictionary of Biblical Theology*, edited by T.D. Alexander, et. al. Leicester, England: InterVarsity Press, 2000.

Vanpelt, M.V., Kaiser Jr. W.C. and Block, D.I. "רוח" *NIDOTTE. Vol-3*, edited by William A. van Gemeren et.al. UK: Paternoster Press, 1996. 1073-1078.

Westermann, Claus. "נפש" *TLOT* Vol. 2, edited by Ernst Jenni & Claus Westermann, translated by Mark E. Biddle. Massachusetts: Hendrickson Publishers, 1977. 743-759.

Zielinski, Lamberty. "נשמה" *TDOT* Vol. X, edited by G. Johannes Botterweck, Heinz-Josef Fabry, translated by Douglas W. Stott. Grand Rapids, Michigan: Eerdmans, 1998. 65-70.

III. Commentaries

Allen, Leslie C. *Ezekiel 20-48: WBC*, edited by David A. Hubbard, et. al. Dallas, Texas: Waco Books, Publisher, 1990.

Binns, L. Elliot. *The Book of the Prophet Jeremiah*. London: SCM Press Ltd., 1919.

Blenknisopp, Joseph. *Ezekiel: Interpretation: A Bible Commentary for Teaching and Preaching*. Louisville: John Knox Press, 1990.

Block, Daniel I. *The Book of Ezekiel 1-24: NICOT*, edited by R.K. Harrison. Grand Rapids, Michigan: Eerdmans, 1997.

Block, Daniel I. *The Book of Ezekiel 25-48: NICOT*, edited by R.K. Harrison. Grand Rapids, Michigan: Eerdmans, 1998.

Bright, John. *Jeremiah: Anchor Bible 21*. Garden City: Doubleday, 1978.

Brownlee, William H. *Ezekiel 1-19 WBC* Vol. 28, edited by David A. Hubbard et. al. Waco, Texas: Word Books, Publisher, 1986.

Brueggemann, Walter. *A Commentary on Jeremiah: Exile and Home Coming*. Grand Rapids, Michigan: Eerdmans, 1998.

Carroll, Robert P. *Jeremiah*. Sheffield: JSOT Press, 1989.

Carroll, Robert P. *The Book of Jeremiah: A Commentary*. Philadelphia: The Westminster Press, 1986.

Clements, R.E. *Jeremiah: Interpretation*, edited by James Luther Mays et. al. Atlanta: John Knox Press, 1988.

Cook, G.A. *The Book of Ezekiel: ICC*. Edinburgh: T&T Clark, 1936.

Cooper Sr., Lotmar Eugene. *Ezekiel: NAC*. Vol. 17, edited by E. Ray Clendenen, et. al. USA: Broadman & Holman Publishers, 1994.

Craigie, Peter C., Kelly Page H. and Drinkard Jr., Joel. *Jeremiah 1-25 Word Biblical Commentary*, edited by David A. Hubbard et. al. Dallas, Texas: Word Books Publisher, 1991.

Darr, Katheryn Pfisterer. "The Book of Ezekiel" *The New Interpreter's Bible Vol. VI*, edited by Leander E. Keck et. al. Nashville: Abingdon Press, 2001.

Davidson, A.B. *The Book of the Prophet Ezekiel.* Cambridge: Cambridge Univ. Press, 1892.

Eichrodt, Walter. *Ezekiel: A Commentary*, translated by Cosslet Quinn. London: SCM Press Ltd., 1970.

George, Adam Smith. *Jeremiah*. London: Hodder and Stoughton, 1929.

Greenberg, Moshe. *Ezekiel 1-20: Anchor Bible* Vol. 20. Garden City, New York: Doubleday & Co. Inc., 1983.

Hanson, Paul D. *Isaiah 40-66: Interpretation*, edited by James Luther Mays et.al. Louisville: John Knox Press, 1995.

Herbert, A.S. *The Book of the Prophet Isaiah Chapters 40-66.* Cambridge: Cambridge Univ. Press, 1957.

Hertzberg, Wilhelm. *I & II Samuel: A Commentary.* Philadelphia: The Westminster Press, 1964.

Holladay, William L. *Jeremiah I.* Philadelphia: Fortress Press, 1986.

_________. *Jeremiah: Spokesman Out of Time.* Philadelphia: United Church, 1974.

Howie, C.G. *Ezekiel, Daniel: Layman's Bible Commentary.* London: SCM Press Ltd., 1961.

Huey Jr., F.B. *Jeremiah and Lamentation: The New American Commentary* Vol.16, edited by E. Ray Clandenen et.al. Nashville, Tennessee: Broadman Press, 1993.

Jones, H. Cunliff. *Jeremiah: God in History.* London: SCM Press Ltd., 1966 (revised edn.).

Keil, Karl Friedrich. *Biblical Commentary of the Prophecies of Ezekiel* Vol. I, translated by James Martin. Edinburgh: T&T Clark, MDCCCLXXVI.

Kelly, Page H. "Isaiah" *Broadman Bible Commentary* Vol. 5, edited by Clifton J. Allen et.al. Nashville: Tennessee: Abingdon Press, 1971.

Keown, G.L., Scalise, P.J. and Smothers, T.G. *Jeremiah 26-52: Word Biblical Commentary.* Dallas, Texas: Word Books, Publisher, 1998.

Knight, G.A.F. *Deutero-Isaiah: A Theological Commentary on Isaiah 40-55*. New York: Abingdon Press, 1965.

Leslie, Elmer E. *Jeremiah Chronologically Arranged, Translated and Interpreted*. New York: Abingdon Press, nd.

Levy, Reuben. *Deutero-Isaiah: A Commentary*. London: Humphrey Milford, 1925.

May, Herbert G. "The Book of Ezekiel: Introduction and Exegesis" *The Interpreter's Bible* Vol. VI, edited by G.A. Buttrick, et. al., Nashville: Abingdon Press, 1956.

McKane, William. *I & II Samuel: Introductory and Commentary*. London: SCM Press Ltd., 1963.

McKenzie, J.L. *Second Isaiah: Anchor Bible*. New York: Doubleday & Company Ltd., 1968.

Miller, Patrick D. "The Book of Jeremiah" *New Interpreter's Bible* Vol. VI, edited by Leander E. Keck et al. Nashville: Abingdon Press, 2001.

Muilenberg, James. "The Book of Isaiah Chapters 40-66: Introduction and Exegesis" *The Interpreter's Bible* Vol. V, edited by G.A. Buttrick et.al. New York: Abingdon Press, 1956.

Nicholson, Ernest W. *The Book of the Prophet Jeremiah 1-25*. Cambridge: Cambridge Univ. Press, 1973.

_________. *The Book of the Prophet Jeremiah 26-52*. Cambridge: Cambridge Univ. Press, 1975.

North, C.R. *The Second Isaiah: Introduction, Translation and Commentary to Chapters XL-LV*. Oxford: Clarendon Press, 1964.

Osswalt, John N. *The Book of Isaiah Chapters 40-66: NICOT*. Grand Rapids: Michigan: Eerdmans, 1998.

Seitz, Christopher R. "The Book of Isaiah" *New Interpreter's Bible* Vol. VI, edited by Leander E. Keck et. al. Nashville: Abingdon Press, 2001.

Skinner, J. *The Book of the Prophet Isaiah Chapters XL-LXVI*. Cambridge: Cambridge University Press, 1917.

Smart, James D. *History and Theology in Second Isaiah: A Commentary on Isaiah 35, 40-66*. Philadelphia: The Westminster Press, MCMLXV.

Stalker, D.M.G. *Ezekiel: Introduction and Commentary*. London: SCM Press Ltd., 1968.

Sweeney, Marvin A. *Isaiah 1-39: With an Introduction to Prophetic Literature*. Grand Rapids, Michigan: Eerdmans, 1996.

Thompson, J.A. *Jeremiah: NICOT*. Grand Rapids, Michigan: Eerdmans, 1980.

Torrey, Charles Cutler. *Pseudo-Ezekiel and the Original Prophecy*. New York: K. Tav Publishing House, Inc., 1970.

_________. *The Second Isaiah: A New Interpretation*. Edinburgh: T & T Clark, 1928.

Toy, C. H. *The Book of the Prophet Ezekiel: A New English Translation with Explanatory Notes*. London: James Clarke & Co., 1899.

Tucker, Gene M. "The Book of Isaiah" *New Interpreter's Bible* Vol. VI, edited by Leander E. Keck et al. Nashville: Abingdon Press, 2001.

Wade, G.W. *The Book of the Prophet Isaiah*. London: Methuen & Co. Ltd., 1929.

Watts, John D. *Isaiah 34-66 WBC* Vol. 25, edited by David Hubbard et. al. Waco, Texas: Word Books Publisher, 1987.

Westermann, Claus. *Isaiah 40-66: A Commentary*. London: SCM Press Ltd., 1969.

Wevers, John W. *Ezekiel: The Century Bible*. London: Thomas Nelson & Sons Ltd., 1969.

Whybray, R.N. *Isaiah 40-66: NCB*, edited by R.E. Clements. London: Oliphants, 1975.

Zimmerli, Walther. *Ezekiel 2: A Commentary on the Book of the Prophet Ezekiel Chapters 25-48*, translated by James D. Martin, edited by Paul D. Hanson with Leo Jay Greenspoon. Philadelphia: Fortress Press, 1983.

IV. Books

Ackroyd, Peter R. *Exile and Restoration: A Study of Hebrew Thought of the Sixth Century*. London: SCM Press Ltd., 1968.

Ackroyd, Peter R. *Israel Under Babylon and Persia*. Great Britain: Oxford University Press, 1970.

Albertz, Rainer. *A History of Israelite Religion in the Old Testament Period Vol. II: From the Exile to the Maccabees*, translated by John Bowden. London: SCM Press Ltd., 1994.

Anderson, Bernhard W. *Understanding the Old Testament*. New Jersey: Prentice-Hall, Inc., 1957.

Andrew, M.E. *Responsibility and Restoration: The Course of the Book of Ezekiel*. Dunedin, New Zealand: University of Otago Press, 1985.

Blenkinsopp, Joseph. *A History of Prophecy in Israel* (revised and enlarged). Louisville, Kentucky: Westminster John Knox Press, 1996.

Brueggemann, Walter. *Hopeful Imagination: Prophetic Voices in Exile*. Philadelphia: Fortress Press, 1986.

__________. *To Pluck Up to Tear Down: A Commentary on the Book of Jeremiah 1-25*. Grand Rapids: Eerdmans, 1988.

Carley, Keith W. *Ezekiel among the Prophets*. London: SCM Press Ltd., 1975.

Carroll, Robert P. *From Chaos to Covenant: Prophecy in the Book of Jeremiah*. New York: Crossroad, 1981.

Childs, B.S. *Introduction to the Old Testament as Scriptures*. Philadelphia: Fortress Press, 1979.

Clements, Ronald E. *Old Testament Prophecy: From Oracles to Canon*. Louisville, Kentucky: Westminster John Knox Press, 1996.

Cowley, A.E. *Gesenius' Hebrew Grammar*, Edited and Enlarged by E. Kautsch. Oxford: Clarendon Press 1910.

Davidson, A.B. *The Theology of the Old Testament*. Edinburgh: T&T Clark, 1907.

_________. *An Introductory Hebrew Grammar* (revised by John Mauchline, 25th edition). Edinburgh: T & T Clark, 1962.

Dheily, Joseph. *The Prophets*. New York: Hawthorn Books, 1960.

Driver, S.R. *Introduction to Literatures of the Old Testament*. New York: Meridian Books, 1956.

Eichrodt, Walter. *Theology of the Old Testament Vol. II*, translated by J.A. Backer. London: SCM Press Ltd, 1967.

Fohrer, George. *History of Israelite Religion*, translated by David E. Green. London: SPCK, 1972.

Goldingay, John. *God's Prophets, God's Servants: A Study in Jeremiah and Isaiah 40-55*. Exeter: The Paternoster Press, 1984.

Heaton, E.W. *The Old Testament Prophets*. London: Darton, Longman & Todd, 1977.

Henry, A.M. *The Holy Spirit*. London: Burns & Oates, 1960.

Hermann, Siegfried. *A History of Israel in the Old Testament Times*. London: SCM Press Ltd., 1975.

Heron, Alsdair I.C. *The Holy Spirit*. Philadelphia: The Westminster Press, 1983.

Holladay, William L. *Isaiah: Scroll of a Prophetic Heritage*. Grand Rapids, Michigan: Eerdmans, 1978.

_________. *Jeremiah a Fresh Reading*. New York: The Pilgrim Press, 1990.

Irwin, W.A. *The Problems of Ezekiel*. Chicago: University of Chicago Press, 1943.

Jacob, Edmond. *Theology of the Old Testament*, translated by Arthur. W. Heathcote and Philip J. Allcock. London: Hodder & Stoughton 1958.

Job, John. *Watchman in Babylon: A Study Guide to Ezekiel*. Exeter: The Paternoster Press, 1983.

Johnson, A. R. *Vitality of the Individual in the Thought of Ancient Israel*. Cardiff: University of Wales Press, 1964.

Joyce, Paul. *Divine Initiative and Human Response in Ezekiel.* Sheffield: Sheffield Academic Press, 1989.

Kapelrud, Arvid S. *Israel from the Earliest Times to the Birth of Christ*, translated by J.M. Moe. Oxford: Basil Blackwell, 1966.

Klein, Ralph W. *Israel in Exile: A Theological Interpretation.* Philadelphia: Fortress Press, 1979.

Laato, Antii. *The Servant of Yahweh and Cyrus: A Reinterpretation of the Exilic Messianic Programme in Isaiah 40-55.* Stockholm: Almqvist & Wiksell International, 1992.

Lampe, G.W.H. *God as Spirit.* Oxford: Clarendon Press, 1977.

Lindblom, Joh. *The Servant Songs in Deutero-Isaiah.* Lund: CWK Glerup, 1951.

Mowinckel, Sigmund. *He that Cometh*, translated by G.W. Anderson. New York: Abingdon Press, 1954.

Mowvley, Harry. *Reading the Old Testament Prophets Today.* Atlanta: John Knox Press, 1979.

Muthunayagom, Daniel Jones. *The Relationship Between Election and Israel's Attitude Towards the Nations in the Book of Isaiah.* Delhi: ISPCK, 2000.

Nicholson, Ernest W. *Preaching to Exiles.* Oxford: Basil Blackwell, 1970.

North, C.R. *The Suffering Servant in Deutero-Isaiah.* Oxford: Oxford University Press, 1959.

Noth, Martin. *The History of Israel.* London: Adam & Charles Black, 1960.

Oesterley, W.O.E. *A History of Israel* Vol. II. Oxford: The Clarendon Press, 1939.

Pfeifer, Robert H. *Introduction to the Old Testament.* New York: Harper & Row Publishers, 1948.

Pritchard, James S (ed). *Ancient Near Eastern Texts Relating to the Old Testament (ANET)*, edited and translated by A. Leo Openheim. Princeton: Princeton Univ. Press, 1955.

Rad, G. von. *Old Testament Theology,* Vol. I. New York: Harper & Row, 1962.

_________. *The Massage of the Prophets.* New York: Harper & Row Publishers, 1965.

Raitt, Thomas M. *A Theology of Exiles.* Philadelphia: Fortress Press, 1977.

Ringgren, Helmer. *Israelite Religion,* translated by David Green. London: SPCK, 1966.

Robinson, H. Wheeler. *The Religious Ideas of the Old* Testament. London: Gerald Duckworth & Co. Ltd., 1956.

_________. *Inspiration and Revelation in the Old Testament.* Oxford: Clarendon Press, 1946.

Robinson, T. H. *Prophecy and the Prophets in Ancient Israel.* London: Gerald Duckworth & Co. Ltd., 1967.

Rowley, H. H. *Man of God: Study in Old Testament History and Prophecy.* London: Thomas Nelson & Sons Ltd., 1962.

Schimdt, Werner H. *Old Testament Introduction,* translated by Matthew J. O'Connell. Bandra, Bombay: St. Paul Publication, 1992.

Schweitzer, Albert. *The Holy Spirit,* translated by H. Reginald and Ilse Fuller. Philadelphia: Fortress Press, 1978.

Scott, E.F. *The Spirit in the New Testament.* New York: George H. Doran Company, 1923.

Sell, Canon. *Prophets of the Exile.* Madras: Diocesan Press, 1923.

Skinner, J. *Prophecy and Religion: Studies in the Life of Jeremiah.* Cambridge: Cambridge Univ. Press, 1930.

Snaith, Norman H. *The Distinctive Ideas of the Old Testament.* London: Epworth Press, 1962.

Stenning, J.F. (ed & trans), *The Targum of Isaiah.* Oxford: Clarendon Press, 1949.

Stuhlmueller, Carroll. *Creative Redemption in Deutero-Isaiah.* Rome: Biblical Institute Press, 1970.

Tucker, Gene M. *Form Criticism of the Old Testament.* Philadelphia: Fortress Press, 1971.

Vriezen, Th. C. *An Outline of Old Testament Theology.* Oxford: Basil Blackwell, 1970.

Weingreen, J. *A Practical Grammar for Classical Hebrew* (Second edn.). Oxford: Clarendon Press, 1959.

Wellhausen, Julius. *Prolegomena to the History of Ancient Israel.* New York: The Meridian Books, 1956.

Whiston. William (trans.). *The Works of Josephus: Complete and Unabridged.* United Sates: Hendrickson Publishers, 1987.

Wilson, Robert R. *Prophecy and Society in Ancient Israel.* Philadelphia: Fortress Press, 1980.

Wolf, Hans Walter. *Anthropology of the Old Testament.* Philadelphia: Fortress Press, 1974.

__________. *Confrontations with Prophets.* Philadelphia: Fortress Press, 1983.

V. Chapters in Books

DeRoche, Michael. "The Spirit Elohim in Gen. 1:2c: Creator or Chaos?" in *Biblical and Other Studies in Memory of Peter C. Craigie*, edited by Lyle Eslinger & Glen Taylor. Sheffield: JSOT Press, 1988.

Dion, Paul E. "Institutional Model and Poetic Creation, the First Song of the Servant of the Lord and Appointment Ceremonies." in *Ascribe to the Lord*, edited by Lyle E., Eliner & Glenn Taylor. Sheffield: JSOT Press, 1988.

Dorfel, Donata. "The Divine Breathing: An Intercultural Investigation of the Holy Spirit." in *Challenges and Responses, Church's Ministry in the Third Millennium: Implications for Theological Education*, edited by Gnana Robinson. Bangalore: ATC, 2000.

Greenberg, Moshe. "Prolegomenon." in *Pseudo-Ezekiel and the Original Prophecy* by Charles Cutler Torrey. New York: Ktav Publishing House, Inc., 1970.

Jones, Edgar. "Exile and Post Exilic Period: 587-175." in *The Bible and History*. London: Lutterworth Press, 1968.

Lang, Bernhard. "Life after Death in the Prophetic Promise." in *Supplement to Vetus Testamentum, Congress Volume: Jerusalem 1986*, edited by J.A. Emerton. Leiden: E.J. Brill, 1988.

Pieters Andre. "The Spirit of God and the Human Spirit." in *The Holy Spirit*, edited by Dow Kirkpatrick. Tidings: Nashville, Tennessee, 1974.

Purdue, Leo G. "Jeremiah in Modern Research." in *A Prophet to the Nation: Essays in Jeremiah Studies,* edited by Leo G. Purdue & Brian W. Kovacs. Winona Lake, Indiana: Eisenbrauns, 1984.

Robinson, H. Wheeler. "Hebrew Psychology." in *The People and the Book*, edited by A.S. Peake. Oxford: Clarendon Press, nd.

Smith, Daniel L. "Jeremiah as Prophet of Non-Violent Resistance." in *The Prophets (A Sheffield Reader),* edited by Philip R. Davies. Sheffield: Sheffield Academic Press, 1999.

VI. Articles in Periodicals

Block, Daniel I. "Gog and the Pouring out of the Spirit: Reflections on Ezekiel XXXIX 21-29." *Vetus Testamentum* 37 (July, 1987): 257-270.

Brueggemann, Walter. "The Book of Jeremiah: Portrait of the Prophet." *Interpretation* XXXVII/2 (April, 1983): 130-145.

Carr, David. "Reaching for Unity of Isaiah." *JSOT* 57 (March, 1993): 61-80.

Clements, R. E. "Beyond Tradition-History: Deutero-Isaianic Development of First Isaiah's Themes." *JSOT* 31 (February, 1985): 95-113.

Clifford, Richard J. "The Unity of the Book of Isaiah and Its Cosmogonic Language." *Catholic Bible Quarterly* 55/1 (Jan. 1993): 1-17.

Coggins, Richard J. "The Exile History and Ideology." *The Expository Times* 110/12 (September, 1999): 389-393.

Haran, Menahem. "From Early to Classical Prophecy: Continuity and Change." *Vetus Testamentum* XXVII/4 (October, 1977): 1-12.

Holladay, William L. "The Years of Jeremiah's Preaching." *Interpretation* XXXVII/2 (April, 1983): 146-159.

Honeycutt, Roy L. "Jeremiah The Prophet and the Book." *Review and Expositor* LXXVIII/3 (Summer, 1981): 303-318.

Lemke, Werner E. "Jeremiah 31:31-34." *Interpretation* XXXVII/2 (April, 1983): 183-187.

Loader, James A. "The Exilic Period in Abraham Kuenen's Account of Israelite Religion" *ZAW* 96/1 (1984): 3-24.

Lust, Johan. "Ezekiel 34-40 in the Oldest Greek Manuscript." *Catholic Bible Quarterly* 43/4 (October, 1981): 517-533.

Luyster, Robert. "Wind and Water: Cosmogonic Symbolism in the Old Testament." *ZAW* 93/1 (1981): 1-10.

Ma, Wonsuk. "The Spirit (Spirit of God) in Isaiah 1-39" *Asian Journal of Theology* 3/2 (October, 1989): 582-596.

Mowinckel, Sigmund. "The Spirit and the Word in the Pre-Exilic Reforming Prophets." *Journal of Biblical Literature* 53 (October, 1934): 199-227.

Owens, John Joseph. "Jeremiah and the Cult" *Review and Expositor* LXVIII/3 (Summer, 1981): 365-379.

Pezhumkattil, Abraham. "Anthropological Concept of Spirit in the Old Testament." *Bible Bhashyam* XVIII/1 (March, 1992): 5-17.

________. "The Spirit as the Power of God in the Old Testament." *Bible Bhashyam* XIX/4 (December, 1993): 283-299.

Seitz, Christopher R. "The Crisis of Interpretation over the meaning and purpose of Exile." *Vetus Testamentum* XXXV/1 (January-March, 1977): 29-34.

Sklba, Richard J. "Until the Spirit from on High is Poured Out on Us (Isa. 32:15): Reflections of the Role of the Spirit in the Exile." *Catholic Bible Quarterly* 46/1 (January, 1984): 1-17.

Thomas, D. Winston, "The Sixth Century B.C.: A Creative Epoch in the History of Israel." *Journal of Semitic Studies* VI/1 (Spring, 1961): 33-46.

Weisman, Ze'ev. "The Personal Spirit as Imparting Authority" *ZAW* 93/2 (1981): 225-234.

Westall, M. R. "The Scope of the Term 'Spirit of God' in the Old Testament." *Indian Journal of Theology* 26/1 (January, 1977): 31-32.

VII. Unpublished Works

Achumi, Nitoy K. "The Meaning and the Use of *Nepes* in the Old Testament and Its Translation into the Sema Naga Bible." Unpublished M. Th. Thesis. Bangalore: UTC, 1975.

Jakob, Sam K. "The Concept of *Spirit* in the Book of Proverbs." Unpublished M. Th. Thesis. Chenai: Gurukul Lutheran Theological College, 1997.

Samuel Raj, J.R. John. "Spirit and Kingship in the Old Testament." Unpublished BD Thesis. Bangalore: UTC, 1983.